Success Is An Inside Job

"Judith Chusid is my secret weapon for transcending barriers to peak creative, financial and personal success in my own life and the lives of my clients. She's brilliant, absolutely fearless and will do whatever it takes to get you there."

Carolyn Alroy, Psy.D.
Psychologist and Performance Coach

"Judith Chusid's strategies are transformational. Day to day challenges become manageable, as big picture goals are achieved. The Inside Job™ provides you with an expansive toolkit that helps you be the best version of yourself."

Eric Gardner
Executive Producer, *Shahs of Sunset*, Bravo TV

"Dr. Chusid's methods are wonderful for jumpstarting all kinds of creative processes in many walks of life. Her insight and practices really work and are exceptional for breaking up all kinds of resistance."

Dennis Broe
journalist, novelist, professor, author,
Birth of the Binge: Serial TV and the End of Leisure

"Judith Chusid has developed an amazing and effective way of helping people to get past their barriers and stuck points when it comes to personal and professional success. This will inspire anyone who wants to enhance their work or creative life."

Ann Smith
Former Executive Director of Breakthrough @ Caron

"I first used the Success Is An Inside Job process to explore a career transition. Then I ended a ten-year relationship and was frozen in pain, anger and resentment. Dr. Chusid helped me work through these feelings to heal and thrive. Today, I have a new life and ideas for a career transition."

Marguerite Schroeder, Esq.
Organizational Development Lawyer

"No one knows how to overcome resistance to change like Judith Chusid. She's got a sound theory for doing that, as well as a huge toolkit. I turn to her for advice in working with our executive clients."

Robert Kaplan
Partner, Kaplan DeVries, Inc.

"Judith Chusid is a rare gem in the field of executive coaching—she combines personal integrity, keen insight, and techniques that have been successful for herself, her company and her clients. She manages to be direct and demanding, while open and engaging at the same time."

Dov Weinstock
President, Salem Global Internet, NYC.

"As athletes and coaches we had been taught not to question each other and never to express our feelings, at least, not without repercussions . . . all of those taboos were broken and our world was turned upside down. She gets the job done . . . ."

Kevin Sheean
"The Chusid Years" in *The History of Adelphi Lacrosse 1948–1994*

Tune into Your Passion * Do What You Love * Follow Your Bliss

SUCCESS IS AN INSIDE JOB

STOP PLAYING SMALL

OVERCOME FEAR OF SUCCESS

LIVE YOUR POTENTIAL

Judith F. Chusid, Ph.D.

Published by: VHM Press
60 West 13th Street
Lobby Suite A
New York, NY 10011

Editorial supervision and book layout: Jaye Manus
Book Cover Design and Graphics: Mary Ann Smith
First Editor: Emily Brewton-Schilling

The author of this book does not dispense medical advice or prescribe the use of any technique as a form of treatment for physical, emotional or medical problems without the advice of a physician, either directly or indirectly. Likewise, the author of this book does not dispense financial advice or prescribe the use of any financial solution without the advice of financial advisors directly or indirectly. The intent of the author is only to offer information of a general nature to help you in your quest for emotional, spiritual, and career well-being. In the event you use any of the information in this book for yourself, which is your constitutional right, the author and the publisher assume no responsibility for your actions.

The author gratefully acknowledges Matina Horner and Donnah Canavan-Gumpert, Katherine Garner, & Peter Gumpert for their formulations and research on the topic of *Fear of Success*.

To the splendor in each of us.

May we live in our potential, do work we love, follow our bliss, and share our gifts with others.

CONTENTS

PART III

THE TOOLKIT:
THE 14 TOOLS FOR SUCCESS

PART IV

SUMMARY AND RESOURCES

ACKNOWLEDGEMENTS

It took ten years to complete this book. When I started writing, I had been resolving fear of success issues for over 35 years, yet I had to overcome my own fears to produce this work. I am forever grateful to everyone in my Inner Circle who supported my journey and believed my work deserved a wider audience.

When I started showing the finished manuscript to outside readers, agents, and marketing consultants, I was told I had a *legacy book*. That is, a book that encompasses experiences gathered over the course of one's career and embraces many people who contributed significantly to that legacy.

To all who have made this book possible and to the students, patients, consulting clients, athletes, coaches, educational institutions, and business organizations who have taken this journey with me, I thank you for trusting me with your resistances and taking a leap of faith that we could overcome them together. I am honored and touched by the work we have done and continue to do. I learned from all of you. I am more enlightened and accurate because of our collaborations.

To Elizabeth Rose, a depth of gratitude. Without you, this book never would have been written. When you first encountered my work, you lovingly nicknamed me the *Suze Orman of Fear of Success*. From that time on, you nagged me relentlessly to write. After months of putting up with my resistance, you finally cajoled me into putting a few words on paper by volunteering to write with me. That was the beginning.

To those who supported my process, gave me feedback and had unconditional belief in my work early on and before publication: Eileen Sanquist Potamos, Jason Grant, Esther and Arje Shaw, Britt Hall, John Swain, Marty Schwimmer and Cathy Simpson, and Daniel Goldstein.

To Dennis Broe, my friend, fellow writer and ally on the journey to self-actualization, you are in my heart always and I say *thank you*. We have known each other for over twenty years, and I am grateful for your support and belief in my work and my writing. I have incorporated your ongoing enthusiasm and feedback into the fabric of my writing process. Most important, thank you for suggesting we form a writer's group. The weekly support from you and our fellow writers has proved invaluable over these last ten years.

To my writers group: Dennis Broe, Dan Kavulish and Mathilde Merlot, without you this manuscript would be imprisoned in my computer. There are no words to express my deep love and appreciation for your belief in me and what I do. I am blessed to have your ongoing friendship, support and love. Each of you is dedicated to writing on a reliable and consistent basis. The works you have produced are inspiring. Your commentary is invaluable, and your guidance is spot on. You all recognized my writer's voice long before I did and long before it developed. Thank you for listening to endless edits and rewrites with patience, grace and insightful feedback. I am grateful for your steadfast commitment to help me complete this book.

To Billy Mowbry and Susan Graves: I so appreciate you cheerleading me through the last two years of edits and publishing. Susan, my friend, creative ally and soul sister for over seventeen years, thank you for your unconditional support, feedback and endless supply of marketing ideas. To Billy, thank you for sharing how the chapters affected you personally.

To Zulema Suarez, thank you for all you have contributed to the Success Is An Inside Job® franchise, including co-facilitating the five-day workshop with me and slogging through edits and giving feedback on the book. You are an incredible wordsmith, writer, clinician and psychodramatist.

To the team that is responsible for putting this book in your hands. Emily Brewton Schilling, my first editor, who loved the book from the beginning, did many more edits than she had planned and successfully applied the principles of the book to her own life. Thank you for shaving off 90 pages. I don't miss those pages and I am sure my readers appreciate a smaller book. To Jaye Manus, my second editor who got the ebook ready and prepared the manuscript for the print version, "Thank you." You are a dream to work with and have made a grueling process very manageable.

To Mary Ann Smith, thank you for designing a book cover I love and for creating the inside charts and illustrations.

To all my mentors in the modern psychoanalytic movement. Extraordinary clinicians, all, who taught me how to identify and resolve resistance. You helped me follow my heart and apply psychoanalytic interventions to problems outside the psychotherapy setting.

To my supervisors in fields of psychiatry, psychology and psychoanalysis, I hold you in light and love. I see clearer and farther because I stood on your shoulders.

To the late William B. Kirman, Ph.D., a debt of gratitude for teaching me how to resolve resistances to learning and behavioral issues in the educational setting. It was that experience I took to sports and later across industry lines.

To the late Hyman Spotnitz, M.D., Ph.D., the father of Modern Psychoanalysis, my mentor, teacher, supervisor and analyst for over 25 years: love, admiration and appreciation. Your commitment to experiment, think out-of-the box and be your authentic self, affected me profoundly. Thank you for recognizing and nurturing my passion and my gift. You taught me to trust my intuition. You encouraged me to keep moving in the direction of my dreams even when I was scared. By example and encouragement, you showed me how to be brave and do the new and the different in service of the better. I miss you on a daily basis.

To the late Ethel Clevans, Ph.D., my beloved analyst, mentor, and psychological mother, thank you. Always the humble genius, your interventions provided me with a unique role model for resolving resistance and holding fast to the frame. Thank you for always believing in me and encouraging me to do my own thing. It served me well. I wish we had more time together. You would be very proud of this work.

To Donna Canavan-Gumpert, Katherine Garner and Peter Canavan for your book, *The Success Fearing Personality*. Your book was published in 1978, the same year I became a sports psychologist. It changed the way I thought and worked. While I had been resolving personal and performance blocks for a number of years, I never identified the problem as *fear of success.* Your book is an important contribution to the field. Thank you.

To Pia Mellody, for your extraordinary contributions to the field of recovery. I embrace your work. Your ideas, concepts and research are a welcome addition to my clinical toolbox.

To Jim Dredge, you are an extraordinary leader and CEO. Thank you for offering my workshop and book a platform. I look forward to launching my book and the Success Is An Inside Job® Workshop with the Rio Retreat Center at the Meadows.

To Todd Whitmer, thank you for embracing the Inside Job approach, bringing me into the Caron family, and facilitating the collaboration between the Success Is An Inside Job® program and Breakthrough at Caron.

To my Cousin Jan Segal, thank you for championing my work, launching the Success Is An Inside Job® Workshop program with me and acting as an informal editor and a daily cheerleader. Your love and unwavering belief in me helped me get to the finish line. To Aliza, David, and Jacob Segal, and Cousin Sara Schoenfeld, thanks for your feedback and support. To my Aunt Helen and beloved late Uncle Stan for your love.

To my dear friends Janet Rotter, Jan Ryan, Stanley Pearlberg, Deb Rubin, Catherine and Peter Johnson and Lauren Dibben, your belief in me makes it possible to produce a work like this.

To Steven A. Marks, thank you for championing my work, the headshots and the feedback you provided over the years.

To Shawn Sprecker, I so appreciate your enthusiastic response to Success Is An Inside Job®, your social media ideas and your persistent campaign to put this book into the hands of my readers.

To Ryan Kull, Ph.D., for your professional enthusiasm, feedback and encouragement to "walk the book out the door." I admire your therapeutic work, value your advice and feel happy you like the manuscript.

To Rabbi Sharon Kleinbaum, for your inspiring and untiring social justice work, spirituality and ability to merge right action with political activism. The spiritual section of this book is greatly enhanced by my work with you and your leadership at CBST. I am forever grateful for your passionate-compassionate dedication to reverse exclusion, disenfranchisement and destructive discourse and action.

To my parents, Phyllis and Harry Chusid, and my brother Barry. I wish you were here, but I know that you share my excitement and joy as this book makes its way into the world. To my mother, thank you for passing on your keen understanding of others and the ability to connect to people in all walks of life. To my father, your intellectual curiosity, spirituality and dedication to right action is imprinted on my soul. To my brother, I learned the challenges of being an identified genius. Your experiences inform my work.

To my beloved late grandmother, Anna Chusid, who lived an incredibly great life. You are my heroine and role model for positivity, compassion, persistence, charitable works and unconditional love. I know you are "kveling" right now and surrounding me with love.

Last and first in my heart, I thank my daughter Victoria Hope. I love you to the moon and back. You enrich my life more than you know. You have a great soul. Your gifts appeared early and you knew what you wanted to do at a young age. Multi-talented, you have been able to use your gifts to perform on stage and help children. Your ability to be compassionate and therapeutic to the infants, children and adolescents in your charge is remarkable. Thank you for being my biggest fan and telling anyone who will listen about my work.

INTRODUCTION

This book addresses a common but rarely discussed life and career block called Fear of Success (FOS). FOS is a psychological conflict that operates below the level of our awareness. In the areas of career and creative endeavors, FOS manifests in myriad ways causing more problems than you can imagine and more trouble than any individual, group or team can cope with on their own.

FOS is complicated because its underlying driver is a deeply rooted conflict in self-esteem, autonomy, and attitudes and beliefs about achieving success. It's particularly destructive because it operates undercover, in the unconscious. An invisible saboteur, it feeds on the unconscious fear and ambivalence we have about achievement and success.

Research[1] shows that people with FOS have a strong conscious desire to succeed and pursue goals and an unconscious unresolved conflict about success that shows up as fear, self-doubt, and ambivalence. This cacophony of emotions presents itself as self-sabotaging behaviors that interfere with work goals and performing on a reliable and consistent basis.

A quote that captures the essence of FOS was written by author, spiritual teacher, social activist, and recent candidate for President of the United States, Marianne Williamson (1992):

> "Our deepest fear is not that we are inadequate. Our deepest fear is that we are powerful beyond measure. It is our light, not our darkness that most frightens us. We ask ourselves, Who am I to be brilliant, gorgeous, talented, fabulous? Actually, who are you not to be? . . . Your playing small does not serve the world. There

---

1 Horner, 1968; Gumpert-Canavan, Garner, Canavan, 1978; Chusid, 1980

is nothing enlightened about shrinking so that other people won't feel insecure around you . . . As we are liberated from our own fear, our presence automatically liberates others."

From: A Return to Love

Holding back in fear and not living up to your potential does not serve you or anyone else.

The Talent Within

I believe we are all born with a gift: an innate talent we are meant to share with the world. Some of us have one special skill; others are multi-talented. When our innate talent makes its first appearance, it emerges as a passionate interest or magnetic pull to engage in a specific kind of activity. This passionate interest contains the seeds of our "right livelihood," (Sinetar, 1989) or what is popularly referred to as *Doing what you love* and *following your bliss*. Steven Pressfield (2002) calls it a "personal destiny" and describes it this way:

> "We come into this world with a specific, personal destiny. We have a job to do, a calling to enact, a self to become. We are who we are from the cradle, and we're stuck with it."

Experience has taught me a thing or two about creating a happy and satisfying work life. When we use our natural talents to do work we love, work has meaning and purpose. I find that doing what I love is essential to my emotional, mental, spiritual and physical health. Finding our calling not only makes us happy, it provides us with an opportunity to share our gifts with others.

Sigmund Freud said, "Love and work are the cornerstones to happiness." If you believe this—and I do—we must nurture our innate abilities and manifest our personal calling.

Many ask, what is the secret to success? The truth is this: *There is no secret to achieving success*. Success is the result of passion, persistence, high courage, faith, and dogged determination. In the words of Winston Churchill:

"Success is going from one failure to another without losing your enthusiasm."

Living in our potential and achieving success is easy if we are conflict-free. In a conflict-free state, we move progressively forward with courage and the determination to face and overcome obstacles. Doing this is difficult, if not impossible, if we're blocked and in our own way. When we're sabotaging ourselves or staying stuck in unhealthy patterns that interfere with or derail us in our careers or creative endeavors, we cannot manifest our dreams or perform at our personal best.

Shrinking because you fear disapproval or feel uncomfortable with others feeling jealous, envious, competitive or angry is an unnecessary personal sacrifice.

How Does FOS Work?

The psychological mechanism that enables FOS to function is an elaborate set of behaviors I call Fear of Success Signals. The FOS Signals are behaviors that interfere with or interrupt momentum as we move along the Success Continuum. Some of us sabotage our efforts in the beginning stages of success, others after achieving a measure of success and a significant number derail after reaching a high level of success. Derailing after reaching the pinnacle of success is called Sabotage at the Top and represents an inability to handle constructively the high visibility, scrutiny, and pressures that accompany success at that level.

FOS is the Enemy of Progress

Do not underestimate FOS! It is the enemy of progress and a formidable opponent operating covertly without your knowledge or permission.

In the FOS scenario, feelings of fear, anxiety and ambivalence are minimized or go unrecognized. This happens outside your awareness, in the unconscious. Before you know it, FOS manifests in one or more of the following ways:

Manifestations of FOS:

- Confusion about your career goal;
- Difficulty creating or manifesting your Vision;
- Underearning;
- Underachieving;
- Workaholism;
- Achieving financial success but feeling unhappy;
- Performing inconsistently;
- Difficulty making a career change or transition;
- Trouble navigating corporate waters;
- Difficulty achieving entrepreneurial goals;
- Sabotage at the Top.

FOS is Like an Iceberg

The psychic structure of FOS resembles an iceberg. The tip, composed of self-sabotaging behaviors and the problems they cause, is visible. The larger part, operating unconsciously, is composed of emotions (fear, anxiety, ambivalence) that conspire to interrupt or distance you from your goals. Just as the ice below the water's surface sank the *Titanic*, FOS can sink your success. Don't let it!

Overcoming FOS is an Inside Job

While getting out of your own way can be a challenging business, my research, clinical practice and consulting experience shows that fear of success can be overcome. As Chaucer said, "You can change your stars." [2]

---

2 "You can change your stars" was written by Geoffrey Chaucer, considered the greatest English Literature Poet of the Middle Ages. It means you can change your circumstances and your life, if you want to and you work at it.

I've learned from personal experience, too. I had to confront my own FOS issues to move forward in my career and to produce this book. While I've been in the success zone for many years, FOS interfered in my life at critical periods.

It raised its ugly head each time I moved from one level on the success ladder to a higher level. There were a number of times in my career where I experienced Sabotage at the Top. I hid in my office for four or five years at a time after experiencing more visibility or a higher level of success.

If you feel you are not living up to your potential and are sabotaging your career or creative endeavors, address the problem now.

About this Book

This book is for everyone. It can change your life if you let it. Whether you are experiencing little or no success, in the beginning stages of creating a career, making a career change or transition, performing inconsistently, struggling to perform at a higher level, or at the top of your game and self-sabotaging, you can start now and make substantial progress.

Don't know what you love to do? You can find your right livelihood and do what you love if you're willing to work at it. If you do know what you love to do, but are underearning, underachieving, performing inconsistently or sabotaging yourself, you can overcome that, too. Even if you're at the top of your field or have reached the pinnacle of success, *Success Is An Inside Job*® can support you and help safeguard your career. Being at the top is a daunting experience, as one of my CEO's describes:

> "All I can say about being at the top, having been the CEO of two multi-billion-dollar corporations, is this—imagine you are climbing the highest summit in the world. As you get close to the top, the air gets thinner and thinner, you need oxygen to survive, the weather is unpredictable, and it can get dangerous. If you survive and reach the top, you realize there's no air, no

safety net, nothing around you. You're alone. It's just you, the breathtaking view, the silence, and miles of sky as far as the eye can see. That's what success is like. Rewarding and lonely."

If you have reached the top of your game and find success "getting to you," don't wait until you start engaging in behaviors that will derail your hard-earned success. Act now! Put tools in place that will prevent a crash. Dispose of the psychological conflicts that have the potential to take you down.

The Inside Job approach and toolkit will help you identify self-sabotaging behaviors and give you the tools to convert those behaviors into constructive action. If you are experiencing confusion about your vision or you are unable to achieve a long-held dream, use the vision exercises to help you move forward.

The information chapters and assessment process will help you understand FOS and discover how it operates in your life. The toolkit will help you create new and healthier career and creative habits. If you don't know your passion, focus on vision work. Vision work will lead you to your right livelihood so you can create work you love.

Surround Yourself with Support

While you can read this book alone and get a lot from it, I strongly recommend you take this journey with a Success Buddy and/or Success Support Group (Chapter 11: Tool 1). We never succeed alone. We all need help. As my friend Marc Friedman says, "Life is a team sport!"

Build a solid circle of support. Your team will help you get to the top of your game and stay there.

To help you stay on track, heed my signature slogan:

> *Your Mind is a Dangerous Neighborhood,*
> *Don't Walk Around Alone.*
> *Get a Success Buddy!*

Bring a Success Buddy or Success Group with you. Your journey will be easier, I promise.

My Story

I was lucky to have found my passion at an early age. The expression "If you love what you do, you'll never work a day in your life," is true for me and it can be true for you, too!

Because I love my work, I am dedicated to helping others get out of their own way, tune into their passion, and do work they love. While the bulk of my time is spent helping individuals, groups, and organizations overcome the psychological blocks that stand in the way of performing at their personal best, I am also devoted to helping people create work they love.

My career has taken me across industry lines, helping people reach optimal performance in business, education, entertainment, fashion, the fine and performing arts, healthcare, non-profit organizations, politics, publishing, sales and sports. The work is exciting and affords me the opportunity to help people manifest their Vision and perform on a reliable and consistent basis.

There are times when we all get in our own way and engage in self-sabotaging behaviors. When we do, we diminish who we are and we interrupt self-actualization. My experience shows that FOS is the main culprit interfering with us living in our potential and manifesting our dreams.

While I believe each one of us is capable of creating work we love and being successful, we must first conquer our limiting beliefs and self-sabotaging behaviors to achieve.

Finding Passion Early

By age four, I was most interested in adult conversations and fascinated with psychological problems. I had a strong desire to help people and readily gave advice to my parent's friends. My desire to help others motivated me to invite the kids in my neighborhood to talk about the problems they were having with their parents, siblings, teachers and friends.

We formed a group that met weekly in the front courtyard of my apartment building and talked about things that bothered us. The kids named the group, "Judith's Circle." I was five and a half.

Mark was the first to present a problem. His mother wouldn't let him wear shorts to school. He was completely undone by her rigidity. While it was a challenge to create a plan that would influence her to change her mind, I encouraged the group to persist. We soldiered through a number of failures, adjusted our strategy, and were delighted when Mark's mother relented and said, "Yes."

The day I recognized my calling was the day Mark told us his mother let him wear shorts to school. It was a defining moment in my life—one I will never forget. That day, Mark was different. He looked handsomer, sat taller, and sounded more confident. I knew we had helped him achieve his goal, and it gave me an inner glow and a deep sense of satisfaction. I remember thinking, "Nothing, absolutely nothing will ever feel better than this—I'm going to do *this* for the rest of my life." While I didn't know what *this* was, I knew for sure I had found my calling and my bliss. I contributed to Mark's happiness and I loved the process.

Despite the fact I was only five and a half years old, the experience with Mark gave me insights into how I functioned naturally and what it took to overcome resistance. While this knowledge operated intuitively in the early years, later I was able to articulate what I knew. Today, these insights are threaded throughout the fabric of my personality and used on a daily basis to help people get out of their own way and perform at their personal best. To resolve resistance, you must:

- Stay focused on solving the problem. To help Mark, we had to resolve his mother's resistance. She was stubborn and refused to see his point of view or ours. There were times the group wanted to give up and move on to another member's problem. I couldn't accept that.

- Be persistent and determined. I am persistent by nature, which is a perfect match for facing and overcoming resistances. While the group felt that Mark's mother represented an insurmountable obstacle, I thought differently. I felt there had to be something we could say that would influence her to change her mind. I had a natural tendency to live by the words (paraphrasing Winston Churchill) "Never, never, never, give up."[3]
- Have faith in the process. I encouraged the group to keep problem solving even when we saw no progress.
- Think out-of-the box and apply what you know. I swam early. My swim teacher constantly said, "Never swim alone, get a buddy." I remembered this and suggested we use the buddy system to help Mark talk to his mother. That suggestion brought me to the last lesson I learned from Judith's Circle:
- Create a solid circle of support. There's power in numbers. "United we stand, divided we fall." I knew Mark should not tackle his mother alone. He needed a buddy or a buddy group.

FAST FORWARD

Twenty-five years later, I became the sports psychologist to the Panthers, Adelphi University's men's lacrosse team, and used the same tenacity and persistence to help Coach Paul Doherty pursue his long-held dream of winning the NCAA National Championship.

At the time, I had no plans to be a sports psychologist. I was in private

---

3 Churchill, Winston, speech at Harrow School, October 29, 1941. nationalchurchillmuseum.org (accessed 8/4/17). What Churchill actually said is: "Never give in, never give in, never, never, never, never, never in nothing great or small, large or petty—never give in except to convictions of honor and good sense."

practice, a full-time instructor at Adelphi teaching psychology courses to undergraduate and graduate education majors, and a consultant to educational institutions. My area of specialization was helping students resolve their resistances to learning and behavioral issues in the classroom. I taught education majors how to help students become successful learners and socializers in the school environment.

An accidental meeting with a professional football coach got me thinking about resolving resistance in the sports arena. The coach was upset with a player who was underperforming. He told me how he was handling the problem and said he was "getting nowhere fast." I gave him some tips and asked if he would let me know how it turned out. He said he would.

Following our meeting, I asked myself: "Could the strategies and interventions I use to resolve resistances in education be applied to a sports setting?" I was so eager to see if the tools I used in the classroom could be applied to sports that I didn't wait to hear from the coach. I went on a mission to find a team that needed my help and would agree to have me.

It was three months before the football coach called to say my advice worked—the player's attitude and performance was improving. By that time, I found in Coach Paul Doherty a willing partner and fellow adventurer at heart. He described his problem this way:

> "I've been trying to win the NCAA Championship for ten years.
> I've taken the Panthers from 64th in Division II to number 8.
> We've been in the playoffs year after year but get eliminated in
> the first round. We have the talent and depth to win, but I can't
> bring my team in. Not sure what the team's resistance or problem
> is, but I think I'm part of the problem. I think I'm in my own way
> but don't know how."

The word *resistance* was music to my ears. I knew winning games depended on resolving any and all resistances that interfere with optimal performance. Paul was willing to experiment with the strategies I had in my toolkit. Together, in the 1978–79 season, we set out to win the NCAA Championship.

I was a double winner when I became the Panthers' sports psychologist. I took my toolkit into the sports arena and was given permission to use my research with the team for my psychoanalytic dissertation. (Chusid, 1980)

It was during the pre-season I observed that FOS was contributing to the team's win-loss record. The team acted out a common FOS signal (behavior): "holding back in fear." They had difficulty scoring when opponents got aggressive. In sports language, they "folded." This interfered with their ability to score goals and sabotaged their winning record. Their inability to harness their aggression constructively in service of winning was the reason they lost games they should have won.

When I told Paul that FOS was at work, he didn't agree. In fact, he felt defensive and offended at the implication. He said, "You're not an athlete. You don't know anything about lacrosse (I didn't), you've never even seen the game before (I hadn't) and now you're telling me my team has an aggression issue and is afraid? That's bullshit!"

The idea that his team was afraid seemed absurd. To help him understand the severity of the team's problem, I gave everyone on register, including Paul and his assistant coaches, a fear of success inventory (Cohen, 1974) and a battery of projective tests.[4] The results spoke volumes. A majority of the players scored high on the FOS inventory, as did Paul and the assistant coaches. I didn't test myself, a mistake it took me years to realize.

Doherty had intuited correctly: he was part of the problem. But how? He couldn't put his finger on it. Those around him had ideas but aside from a theory here or there, they were puzzled, including other coaches who knew Paul well.

After all, Paul had been a star defenseman inducted into the Lacrosse Hall of Fame. He held records. As a coach, he was touted as an ingenious

---

4 Projective Psychological Tests are designed to reveal hidden emotions and internal conflicts. The individual taking the test is exposed to ambiguous stimuli-like pictures, ink blots and drawings. What the individual "projects" onto these non-specific stimuli are various attitudes, feelings and thoughts that can be analyzed. The team was given the Thematic Apperception Test, the Rorschach, Sentence Completion, and the Draw-A-Person.

strategist. Those who knew him said, "Doherty knows lacrosse and recruits talented athletes who want to win."

Therein lies the problem. The team's conscious desire to win *versus* their unconscious conflict. On the conscious level, Paul and the team wanted to win games. On the unconscious level, FOS was interfering with the team's ability to do that. Holding back in fear was the most visible FOS symptom, but it wasn't the only one. They also misused their aggression in a variety of other ways.

The interventions I created for the educational setting transferred successfully to sports, with a tweak here and there. Our experiment worked: the Panthers won the 1979 NCAA National Championship.

I stayed on as the team's sports psychologist for another four years. During my five-year tenure with the Panthers, Paul and I produced one winning season after another. The team was also the first in sports history to move from Division II to Division I. Doherty acknowledged our work and expressed his gratitude by naming a chapter in his book, "The Golden Age of Lacrosse—The Chusid Years." (Doherty, 1994)

I'm very grateful to Paul and the team for allowing me to work with them. Being the Panthers' sports psychologist set the stage for the work I've been doing for over forty years.

Now, decades later, I have resolved many of my own fear of success issues and I am still helping individuals, groups and organizations resolve theirs. I might add that it's easier to help others than myself. However, persistence works, and success is imminent if you keep at it.

SUCCESS IS AN INSIDE JOB® WORKSHOPS

In 2011, thirty-two years after I entered sports, I launched Success Is An Inside Job®, Inc. (SIIJ), a consulting practice that focuses on resolving career blocks and FOS issues. Building on years of experience across industry lines, SIIJ offers assessment services, career counseling, performance enhancement and executive coaching, and a five-and-a-half-day residential workshop.

In the residential workshop setting, participants have an opportunity to "unplug" from the outside world and focus on themselves. Attendees work on a variety of issues: recognizing self-sabotage; identifying career blocks; exploring their passion; creating or recommitting to a Vision; and designing an action plan for moving forward. We immediately assign everyone a Success Buddy and Spiritual Partner. Everyone leaves with a thirty-day action plan.

Over the last nine years, we have helped hundreds of participants identify FOS and how it operates in their lives. Attendees create short-term and long-term plans to help them reach their goals.

Our tag line reads: One Week Can Change Your Life. By that we mean, that one week can change your perspective and heighten your awareness. One week can help you identify your resistances and clarify the self-sabotaging behaviors that prevent you from achieving your goals. For those who want to focus on Vision issues, the workshop can help you clarify or recommit to your Vision.

While a week can open your eyes and change your point of view, overcoming FOS involves follow-up and focused work. To make progress and reap the benefit of substantial changes you must be willing to take action on a reliable and consistent basis.

This book contains strategies I use in my practice and exercises created specifically for the SIIJ workshop. Clients and attendees find these helpful. If you use them in conjunction with the toolkit, you will develop healthier habits. If you work at it, the Inside Job approach will help you resolve self-sabotage and live in your potential.

Psychological Debris

Thinking about resistance, it occurs to me that I've been in the waste management business all these years. I help people who are motivated and willing to do the work dispose of the psychological debris undermining their lives. The bulk of this debris is composed of resistances to success and FOS issues.

If I had given myself the FOS scale I gave the Panthers, I would have realized much earlier in my career that I too was held back by FOS. Looking back, it is evident that FOS had been operating in my personality since childhood. It was subtle but it was there. Don't let that happen to you.

It's Never Too Early or Too Late to Do What You Love

While stories about childhood prodigies, mine included, can be engaging and instructive, it doesn't make us immune to FOS issues. In fact, FOS can be easily missed by the "Wow factor." I know it was with me.

And, remember that many of us do not find our bliss when we're young. Whether that's because FOS is operating or other factors come into the mix, I can't say. I do have theories but that's for another book.

If you haven't found your bliss, don't be discouraged. I personally know people who have found their life's work at the age of sixty and older. We all have the potential to tune into our passion and convert our passion into work we love.

More importantly, this applies to FOS, as well. It's never too late to get out of your way and follow your bliss. The only tragedy is if you never pursue it.

Success Is An Inside Job® **will:**

- Teach you how to work with a Success Buddy and a Success Group so you have support in your journey.
- Encourage you to nurture your spiritual side and work with a Spiritual Partner.
- Help you identify if FOS is sabotaging your work life.
- Help you understand FOS and how it operates.
- Provide you with tools and strategies to overcome FOS.
- Help you tune into your passion.
- Help you create a vision.
- Support you to do what you love and follow your bliss.

- Show you how to create an action plan that incrementally moves you toward your goals.

Don't waste any time. Get a Success Buddy and make a beginning!

My Vision for You

If you have an awareness that there is something more inside you waiting to break free, listen to your inner voice. It is counseling you to be the most authentic expression of who you are.

I have been doing what I love and following my bliss for more than forty years and I highly recommend it. I also work on overcoming my own fears and psychological blocks. You can too! All you need is the desire to change, a solid support system and the willingness to try something different.

The expression "if you do what you've done, you'll get what you got" applies here. Do not recycle solutions that haven't worked. That's a recipe for failure. Refresh your problem-solving button and take a new approach to your work life.

I suggest you read this book with a Success Buddy, create a solid support system and find your spiritual center. Do the exercises and use the toolkit. If you do, by the time you finish this book, you'll be out of your own way and happily heading in a new direction.

My vision for you is that you overcome fear of success, live in your potential and create work you love.

I wish you an exciting journey of self-discovery and self-growth.

Let's get started!

Warmest regards,
Dr. Judith F. Chusid

PART I

THE PROBLEM:
FEAR OF SUCCESS

CHAPTER 1

What is Fear of Success?

"Most of us live two lives. The life we live, and the unlived life within us. Between the two stands Resistance . . . Resistance is the most toxic force on the planet . . . To yield to resistance deforms our spirit. It stunts us and makes us less than we are and were born to be."

Steven Pressfield,
The War of Art (2002)

What is Success, Anyway?

Success means different things to different people. There may be as many definitions of success as there are people. The Merriam-Webster dictionary defines it as "a favorable or desired outcome; or the attainment of wealth, favor or eminence."

Past high achievers described success:

- Winston Churchill believed success was about being relentless. He said, "Success is going from failure to failure without losing your enthusiasm."
- Stephen Covey described success as "deeply individual" and

believed, "If you carefully consider what you want said of you in the funeral experience, you will find your definition of success."

- Maya Angelou connected success with self-esteem and enjoying your work. She said, "Success is liking yourself, liking what you do, and liking how you do it."

Current high achievers have varying perspectives on the subject of success:

- Deepak Chopra equates success with constant growth. In his book, The Seven Laws of Spiritual Success, he writes, "Success in life could be defined as the continued expansion of happiness and the progressive realization of worthy goals."
- Richard Branson believes success is about engagement. He said, "The more you're actively and practically engaged, the more successful you will feel."
- Oprah Winfrey believes success is about staying close to your mission and being totally present. J.J. McCorvey (2015) describes the key to Oprah's success as "radical focus." When David Letterman asked Oprah how she felt about failing at the O channel for years, Oprah said, "Never count Oprah out!" The implication is that Oprah believes success is accomplished through determination, persistence, and dedication to the goal.

What do these high performers have in common? What is abundantly clear is that they're all not only interested in accomplishing their goals but also have the passion and determination to keep moving forward. Each has a history that explains his or her motivations. They are also happy doing what they do, which brings me to the next important concept about success: we are happiest when we do what we love and live in our potential.

HAPPINESS AND SUCCESS

In her book, *Do What You Love, The Money Will Follow*, Marsha Sinetar (1989) writes:

> "When you study people who are successful, it is abundantly clear that their achievements are directly related to the enjoyment they derive from their work. They enjoy it, in part, because they are good at it . . . Right Livelihood is an idea about work, which is linked to the natural order of things. It is doing our best at what we do best. The rewards that follow are inevitable and manifold . . . Any talent we are born with eventually surfaces as a need . . . Right Livelihood is the natural expression of this need."

Looking at career and creative endeavors from the standpoint of doing what you love, I define success as:

- Doing work you love in an environment that affirms your talent, skills and abilities;
- Earning an income commensurate with your experience, expertise and work ethic;
- Working in an environment that nurtures you emotionally, intellectually, creatively and spiritually.

SUCCESS IS ACCOMPLISHED IN STAGES

It is important to remember that success is achieved incrementally. Think of success as any action, accomplishment or achievement that moves you toward your goal and helps you self-actualize.

Success Is An Inside Job®

Success starts from the inside and works its way to the outside. When you do the Inside Job, you turn inward for answers. When you turn inward, you give up thinking someone else can help you identify your passion or tell you what you love to do. You realize that your mother, father, partner, best friend, children, colleague, mentor or guru cannot unlock your potential.

When you commit to doing the work, you find answers that are uniquely yours. This is an internal process and a personal commitment to the journey of self-actualization. The Inside Job becomes your responsibility. You learn that no one can think for you. You're the only person who can identify your passion. Only you can name and claim your purpose and only you can turn your passion into creative action.

When you do the Inside Job, you uncover answers that are unique to you. You come to understand your passion and see that you are unique. While it seems a cliché, the truth is there is only one *you* on the planet. No one else will think, perform, or create exactly as you do. This awareness is a blessing and a challenge.

Honor your unique gifts. Make a commitment to live up to your potential. Stop playing small. Do not engage in behaviors that will interfere with your hard-earned success. Start doing the Inside Job by identifying your FOS behaviors and overcoming them. Then tune into your passion and convert it into creative action.

Finding Your Passion

Doing what you love is driven by passion. Passion is inborn and arises from deep within us. It surfaces on its own when we display our natural talents, skills and abilities. Passion contains the seeds of our calling—our purpose. I truly believe we are born with a calling and that we all have a job to do while we are on the planet Earth. It's in our DNA. It's our gift to the planet. Our job is to nurture our gift and share it with others.

Passion reveals itself as focused energy and interest and a strong desire to take certain actions. You don't have to push or prod it. It emerges on its own and in *its own time*—if it's not discouraged or prohibited.

It's never too late to tune into your passion. Deepak Chopra was already a doctor when he awoke to his passion and began to focus on spirituality. A friend of mine found her passion at 65. After thirty-five years in business, she realized she wanted to be a therapist. She went back to school and earned an M.A. in social work. Today, at 73, she is in private practice and loving it.

ARE YOU IN YOUR OWN WAY?

Getting out of your own way is the key to succeeding at the Inside Job. Tuning into your passion and turning your passion into creative action is a natural, conflict-free process—unless someone or something disturbs the natural flow. Sabotage can come from outside or inside. Outside saboteurs can come in the form of economic conditions or industry fluctuations or people who have negative intentions.

When economic conditions or industry fluctuations threaten your livelihood, you need resilience and creativity to address what is happening and a solid commitment to make the changes necessary to meet those demands. When people try to sabotage your performance or work status because they feel jealous, critical, or judgmental, you need emotional support and a good set of strategies to confront the circumstances.

Any form of sabotage makes it difficult to pursue your passion and perform on a reliable and consistent basis. Outside circumstances can interfere in our lives. We have little control over economic conditions and industry changes that force us to rethink how we are going to use our talents and skills.

When it comes to people who are not supportive or, worse, have negative intentions, we need to problem-solve, think out-of-the-box and create ways to overcome those circumstances. It helps to get advice and support, stay positive and adopt a can-do attitude.

FOS saboteurs are another matter. They are internal and toxic. Common saboteurs from the inside are fear and self-doubt. These emerge from a harsh Inner Critic so many of us carry deep within our psyches. Fear and self-doubt are particularly lethal. They chip away at your ambition and confidence. They play havoc with your Vision and dampen your desire to pursue your dream.

Defining Fear of Success

FOS is feeling uncomfortable or anxious about achieving success. This happens outside your awareness, in your unconscious. It represents a psychological conflict characterized by a strong desire to move toward what you want and an equally strong desire to move away from what you want.

This push-pull creates ambivalence toward achieving success and sets in motion behaviors that sabotage the flow of progress. FOS has the power to get you to play small, interrupt your momentum, or sabotage yourself once you've reached the top of your game.

If you think FOS may be operating in your life, answer these questions:

- Am I living up to my potential?
- Am I doing what I love or just earning a paycheck?
- Am I underusing or overusing my strengths?
- Do I have a history of performing inconsistently?
- Am I at the top of my game and engaging in behaviors that have the potential to ruin or derail my career?
- Am I derailing right now?

If you answered "Yes" to any of the above, FOS may be your problem.

More About Fear of Success

FOS is a resistance to success. When active, it stops you from performing reliably and consistently and gets you to engage in behaviors that sabotage your goals.

While FOS is common and operates all around us, it is rarely identified or called by its true name: Fear of Success. Daily, the media gives us a front-row seat into the self-destructive behaviors of celebrities and public figures. And, thanks to reality TV, we can also watch how self-sabotage operates in everyday people who allow cameras to follow their every move.

Closer to home, we can see FOS at work in our family members, friends, coworkers and acquaintances. We watch them act self-destructively and do things that move them away from their goals. This is FOS in action. Observing this, we feel frustrated and puzzled. We ask, "What would motivate anyone to act like that?"

As a qualitative researcher, clinician and performance consultant, I have seen the insidious way FOS operates. It is a sneaky mischief-maker that can strike anywhere on the Success Continuum. Stealth-like, it operates without your knowledge or permission.

It may surprise you to learn who has struggled with it. Take actress Eva Mendes as an example. In an interview with *Gotham* magazine (October 2007), Mendes confided she had fear of success. She described it this way:

Eva Mendes: I started going to therapy a year ago, and I love it. I wasn't dealing with fame very well. I wasn't comfortable being recognized, so I thought, well, this is as good a time as any to go. I think everybody needs therapy or some form of guidance.

Gotham: Did you learn anything about yourself that really surprised you?

EM: Yes—that on some level I have a fear of success. I've always been a go-getter, saying, "I'm going to do this, I'm going to do that, and I'm going to rise above." So, it was like, "No, I can't have a fear of success, I'm so ambitious!" I was shocked. But then I looked at my actions—not going to certain places, even Disney World with my family, not doing certain things. Always wanting to just hang out at friends' houses . . . that sort of thing.

Writer Fran Lebowitz (2010) reported a similar discovery about how FOS manifested in her life. In Martin Scorsese's documentary about her career, *Public Speaking,* she shared this insight with the film's interviewer:

Interviewer: Your first book was a best seller. You got a big book deal to write a second book and then you didn't write for ten years. Why? Were you in writer's block?

Fran: Writer's block is when you don't write for a week, a month. Ten years is a writer's blockade.

Interviewer: Why?

Fran: Isn't it obvious? I had a fear of success.

Mendes, like so many people I have interviewed and worked with over the years, found it hard to believe that FOS was driving her behaviors. Lebowitz, however, understood what was blocking her. Mendes and Lebowitz are two very different people manifesting FOS in different ways.

Once we bring FOS into the open, it is easier to see that it is a driving force behind all kinds of career blocks.

A Closer Look at FOS

In the field of psychology, FOS is considered an approach-avoidance conflict. The psychology is simple: achieving success feels desirable and achieving success feels scary. This creates ambivalence.

How does the psyche deal with ambivalence? With FOS, the psyche lets the conscious mind lead the way. On a conscious level, you focus on acknowledging your potential and your strong desire to achieve. The feelings of fear and discomfort associated with success get pushed out of consciousness with the help of defenses like denial, repression or reaction formation. Therefore, the fear you have about achieving success happens outside your awareness.

This conflict creates a psychic battle between the conscious and the unconscious mind. The conscious mind encourages you to move forward. The unconscious mind creates a game plan to move you away from your goals. This intra-psychic battle between the desire to reach for success and the desire to back away from success creates an approach-avoidance conflict.

Kurt Lewin, (1935) one of the founders of modern social psychology, was the first to identify this conflict. In 1935, he described the approach-avoidance conflict as one where a single goal or event has both positive and negative characteristics, making the goal simultaneously appealing and unappealing. In its grip, we move with great vigor and excitement toward the desired goal until we become increasingly aware of its downside. When this happens, fear and anxiety surface. At that point, the unconscious takes charge and seduces us into engaging in behaviors that will sabotage our performance or momentum.

I call these sabotaging behaviors "FOS Signals" because they provide us with an alert that FOS is operating. While the FOS conflict is invisible, the FOS Signals (behaviors) are visible and tangible. They leave a trail of destruction.

The FOS pattern is riddled with ambivalence about visibility, achievement and success. The ambivalence gets acted out in myriad ways, taking up psychic space that depletes emotional and intellectual energy and interferes with creativity.

THEORIES ABOUT FEAR OF SUCCESS

Sigmund Freud was the first to introduce the idea that some people are "wrecked by success." In an early paper, he described two patients who destroyed their lives after achieving hard-earned success. He called them "the exceptions" and wrote, "It seems as though they were not able to tolerate their happiness." (Freud, 1914–1916)

Since that time, clinicians have come to understand that the problem is not an inability to tolerate happiness, as Freud first thought, but rather about an inability to face, manage or overcome various anxieties and fears associated with achieving a goal or reaching a significant level of visibility or success. Those who reach the top of their game and self-destruct are victims of Sabotage at the Top.

A number of clinical researchers and theorists have discussed the FOS syndrome and proposed explanations to questions like, "What is the etiology of fear of success?" and "How does it operate?" Matina Horner, a pioneer in FOS, published an article in *Time* magazine based on her dissertation findings (1972) on the subject. It was actually Horner who put the phrase "fear of success" on the map.

Another breakthrough came in 1978, when a team of three university professors, Canavan-Gumpert, Garner and Gumpert, published *The Success-Fearing Personality: Theory and Research*. They concluded that the seeds of FOS are planted early—during childhood or adolescence. In those early years, when the children or adolescents displayed individuation, autonomy, and their unique brand of creativity, they were met by parents, significant figures or society with ambivalence, negativity or a double message about success.

These messages in the individuals' histories resulted in success becoming associated with positive *and* negative experiences or consequences. The positive experiences brought joy, excitement, and opportunities to gain personal satisfaction from attaining goals. The negative experiences or consequences created fear, shame or guilt, and sometimes all three.

Canavan-Gumpert, Garner and Gumpert's research identified key personality traits associated with the "success-fearing" personality. These are: low and unstable self-esteem, a preoccupation with being evaluated, a tendency to devalue accomplishments, a tendency to become anxious when close to success, and a pattern of engaging in self-sabotaging behaviors before or after reaching the goal.

My research and clinical work (Chusid, 1980) reveal similar findings with some interesting twists. Individuals with FOS are naturally gifted, have a strong desire to achieve, and work in a competitive arena. For the most part, individuals with FOS are not hiding in their bedrooms.

However, no matter how talented or successful they are, at the core of their personalities rests vacillating self esteem, fear and discomfort with disapproval and a fear of people feeling angry, jealous, or competitive with their success. In addition, individuals with FOS are extremely sensitive to toxic envy and begin to under- or over-perform in the presence of people who have those feelings.

In my experience, individuals with FOS tend to fall into two major groups: 1) those who perform inconsistently and have trouble reaching the top of their game; and 2) those who perform at a high level and sabotage themselves after they achieve success.

Here is a more in-depth view of my findings:

INCONSISTENT PERFORMERS

- Were identified in childhood or adolescence as talented with the potential to be successful.
- Have a history of inconsistent performance (for some, as early as elementary school) often accompanied by up and down earnings in adulthood.
- Have vacillating self-esteem.
- Fear disapproval and negative judgment.
- Fear criticism, even if it is in service of improving performance.
- Fear anger, jealousy, envy and competitive behavior.
- Tend to under- or overvalue their accomplishments.
- Tend to over- or underperform (under- or overcompensate) in the face of toxic envy.
- Feel ambivalent about achieving success.
- Have a history of self-sabotage that interrupts the actual occurrence of success or ruins the enjoyment of achieving it.

HIGH PERFORMERS

- Were identified early as having the talent to be successful.
- Have a history of high performance, often from a young age.
- Have self-doubt despite a history of performance success.
- Have a lack of self-confidence that does not match their achievement history.
- Tend to seek approval and become anxious and worried when approval is not forthcoming.
- Are highly focused on achieving their goal.

- Are perfectionistic, often with harsh Inner Critics.
- Tend to feel anxious when they reach success and struggle with handling the pressures of success.
- Tend to engage in behaviors that reduce or medicate anxiety and also have the potential to derail success.
- At the extreme, there's a tendency to engage in behaviors that can prove fatal.

Assess with a Success Buddy

Not sure if FOS is your problem? Use the checklists in Chapter 2: Do You Have Fear of Success? to assess yourself. And, as you get ready to engage in the assessment process, think about inviting someone to be your Success Buddy. Turn to Chapter 11: Tool 1 for some ideas on how to do this.

FOS is sneaky and powerful and difficult to overcome alone. The process is easier with a Success Buddy or trustworthy person who is supportive!

Do You Have
Fear of Success?

The Self-Assessment Process

This chapter is designed to help you discover if FOS is operating in your life. If you give them a chance, the FOS checklists and graphs will heighten your awareness about how FOS works and the impact it has on your achievements.

Pay close attention to the FOS Signals Checklist. Each signal represents a specific behavior that sabotages achievement. And each signal can be identified and tracked.

The charting exercises on school and work achievement will give you a clear and graphic picture of your achievement history from childhood to the present.

After you complete the self-assessment, you should be able to recognize if FOS is interfering in your career and creative endeavors. Because we are human, it is hard to maintain a high level of performance reliably and consistently without some interference. These assessment tools will shed light on how FOS is dampening your Vision, preventing you from living in your potential or interfering with or derailing your career. In totality, the assessments will provide you with a lifetime achievement inventory.

How to Approach the Assessment Process

Check the statements that apply to you from both checklists. While people invariably fall into one category or the other, most of us find we can relate to statements from both lists. The self-assessment process will nudge your memory. Check a statement or signal even if you engage in it periodically. To get the most mileage from the assessment process, be rigorously honest.

The FOS Checklist for Inconsistent Performers

Circle the statements that apply to you and tally your score at the bottom. Then do the exercise that follows. If two or more of the statements apply, FOS may be the cause of your inconsistent performance.

1. I have been told all my life that I have the potential (talent, skill, creativity) to be successful.
2. I have a history of self-sabotage when I am close to my goal or after I achieve some measure of success.
3. I feel anxiety on a regular basis.
4. I have a history of underachieving.
5. I have a history of underearning.
6. I have a history of up-and-down earnings.
7. I behave in ways that short-circuit goals and hinder my success.
8. I resent having to take care of myself and want to be taken care of.
9. I deny reality and live in a fantasy.
10. I fear disapproval.
11. I find it difficult to ask for and accept help.
12. I sabotage myself by engaging in addictions, codependency, compulsive behaviors or perfectionism.

13. I dream and talk about plans that I do not manifest.
14. I do not believe I can succeed.
15. I suffer from self-doubt or shame, even when I'm succeeding.
16. I have trouble envisioning my career path.
17. I have trouble committing to goals, projects and people.
18. I have difficulty clarifying my Vision (what I love to do—the job, career or creative path I should follow).
19. I feel stuck and can't make the career transition I want.
20. I know what I love to do, but don't believe I can earn a prosperous living doing it.

Number of statements identified ___/20

EXERCISE: Create a chart. For each statement that applies to you, list it and give an example (similar to the sample below):

Statement	Illustrate with examples from your life.
9. I deny reality and live in fantasy.	I decided that I didn't have to advertise or market my café. I imagined that people would just come by word-of-mouth, or my friends and acquaintances would drum up business without my doing anything. As a result, my café is not thriving financially.

THE FOS CHECKLIST FOR HIGH PERFORMERS

Circle the statements that apply to you and tally your score at the bottom. Then do the exercise that follows. If three or more of the statements apply, FOS may be sabotaging your performance.

1. I have a history of achievement.
2. I have an excellent work ethic and consider myself a hard worker.
3. I suffer from self-doubt even though I have been a high performer all my life.

4. I question whether I deserve the success I have.
5. I frequently feel anxious.
6. I am a perfectionist.
7. I frequently have a severe inner voice berating, advising or criticizing me.
8. I feel best about myself when I'm achieving.
9. I tend to feel grandiose and arrogant when I'm successful.
10. I need and seek positive feedback.
11. I ask myself, "Is this all there is?"
12. I like the drama and intensity of work.
13. I find it difficult to relax, preferring to work.
14. I feel depressed when I stop working.
15. I am a workaholic and I like it.
16. My strongest sense of identity comes from my job, career or creative endeavors.
17. I feel that without my work I have no identity.
18. I am successful but feel unhappy.
19. I feel stuck and can't make the career change or transition I want.
20. I engage in behaviors that have the potential to sabotage my career.

Number of statements identified ___/20

EXERCISE: Create a chart. For each statement that applies to you, list it and give an example (similar to the sample below):

Statement	Illustrate with examples from your life.
7. I frequently have a severe inner voice berating, advising or criticizing me.	My "task-master" Inner Critic tells me I'm lazy and should work harder. My "underminer" Inner Critic weakens my confidence and challenges my competence.

The FOS Signals Checklist

DEFINITION

FOS Signals are feelings, thoughts, attitudes and behaviors that go into action when you feel afraid, uncomfortable, ambivalent or pressured by achievement. Each Signal interrupts your momentum and puts distance between you and your goal.

Characteristics of the FOS Signals

- Each signal can be identified and is visible.
- Each signal can be tracked. You can count the frequency and intensity of the ones you use.
- Each signal falls into one of two categories: emotional (feelings) or cognitive (thoughts, attitudes, beliefs).
- Each signal can be active or passive.

Once you tune into the FOS Signals you habitually use, you can follow how they operate. Experiment with tracking them on a daily, weekly, or monthly basis. Tracking your FOS Signals gives you a baseline and helps to shine a light on a process that has been operating unconsciously for a long time. Embrace your FOS Signals. Accept and own them.

HOW TO APPROACH THE FOS SIGNALS CHECKLIST

Take your time. Check each Signal you use. FOS Signals are important because they run the show.

1. Read each category and Signal carefully.
2. Be rigorously honest.

3. Check the Signals you use even if you engage in the behavior infrequently.

THE FOS SIGNALS CHECKLIST

Check the box next to each Signal that applies to you. Tally your score at the bottom. Then do the exercise that follows.

ESTEEM ISSUES

- ❏ I feel inferior or superior to others.
- ❏ I use money or status to feel better about myself.
- ❏ I get into the compare/despair game.
- ❏ I feel anxious or uncomfortable when I'm in the spotlight.
- ❏ I have difficulty asking for or accepting help.
- ❏ I devalue or overvalue my abilities, talents, or skills.
- ❏ I take things personally.
- ❏ I over- or undervalue my accomplishments.
- ❏ I need to achieve to feel valuable and worthwhile.

FEAR

- ❏ I procrastinate.
- ❏ I need to do things perfectly.
- ❏ I feel afraid (infrequently, sometimes, often).
- ❏ I hold back in fear.
- ❏ I feel anxious (infrequently, sometimes, often).
- ❏ I feel overwhelmed (infrequently, sometimes, often).
- ❏ I fear authority figures and act invisible, defiant or compliant.
- ❏ I fear negative judgment, criticism, and disagreement.
- ❏ I fear disapproval.
- ❏ I experience lack of praise as disapproval, rejection or abandonment.
- ❏ I feel afraid when people feel angry, jealous, envious or competitive towards me.
- ❏ I fear failure and success.

- ❑ I fear being happy; something bad might happen.
- ❑ I act impulsively regarding work issues.
- ❑ I over- or undersell due to anxiety, self-doubt or lack of self-confidence.

Performance Issues

- ❑ I have inconsistent work or performance patterns.
- ❑ I tend to have poor or no follow-up around work or creative endeavors.

Resentment, Anger and Frustration Issues

- ❑ I feel critical and judgmental of others.
- ❑ I have difficulty being a team player.
- ❑ I have low frustration tolerance.
- ❑ I need to be in control.
- ❑ I resent the success of others.
- ❑ I resent being told what to do.
- ❑ I resent having to take care of myself.

Money Issues

- ❑ I overspend or scrimp.
- ❑ I have an illogical relationship with money.
- ❑ I constantly worry about money.
- ❑ I have deprivation mentality.
- ❑ I hoard money personally or in business.
- ❑ I do not know how to live abundantly.
- ❑ I am successful financially, but unhappy.

Vision Issues

- ❑ I have a clear Vision but can only manifest part of it.
- ❑ I have difficulty creating a clear Vision.
- ❑ I feel ambivalent toward my job or business.
- ❑ I have difficulty making a career transition or job change.
- ❑ I do not know how to earn a living doing what I love.

Distraction Issues

- ❑ I become distracted by people, places, things, and projects.
- ❑ I turn my focus to infatuations that adversely affect my work performance.

Denial & Blame Issues

- ❑ I tell myself, "I don't have a problem."
- ❑ I make excuses or rationalize my work issue.
- ❑ I blame others for my problems with success.
- ❑ I feel that life has dealt me a "wrong" hand.

Self-Criticism

- ❑ I tell myself, "I don't know if I can do it."
- ❑ I ask myself, "Who am I to achieve this?"
- ❑ I give myself negative advice, such as, "I should just give up on this because it will never happen."
- ❑ I have a recurring thought: "Success only happens for other people, not me."

Spiritual Depletion

- ❑ I do not have a spiritual practice.
- ❑ I do not feel spiritually present.
- ❑ I want to be rescued.
- ❑ I am not seeking an inside solution.

Ambivalence about Moving Forward

- ❑ I know for sure FOS is my problem, but I feel ambivalent or defiant about facing it and taking action.
- ❑ I ask myself whether success is worth all this work.
- ❑ I work at overcoming fear of success inconsistently.

My Personal FOS Signals

Make a list of any additional feelings, thoughts, attitudes, or behaviors you engage in that are not on the FOS Signals list above.

❏ _____
❏ _____
❏ _____
❏ _____
❏ _____

Total number of signals identified _____

EXERCISE: Create a chart. List all the Signals that apply to you, and give examples (similar to the sample below):

My Profession	FOS Signal	Illustrate with examples from your life.
Wealth Manager for the ABC Bank	Procrastination *and* I engage in the compare/ despair game	I delay calling my clients *and* I avoid doing paperwork. *and* When the monthly stats are published, I lose a day or two of work comparing myself to others.

The Success Continuum

The Success Continuum, as I conceptualize it, is composed of five levels of success:

LEVEL 1: Make a beginning
LEVEL 2: Move out of the gate
LEVEL 3: Achieve and make progress

LEVEL 4: Move up the success zone

      STAGE A: Beginning success

      STAGE B: Intermediate success

      STAGE C: Advanced success

      STAGE D: Ongoing success, moving to the top

LEVEL 5: Top of your game

THE SUCCESS CONTINUUM

Beginning * Out of the Gate * Achievement & Getting Ahead * Success Zone (beginning, intermediate, advanced, ongoing) * Top of Your Game

FOS AND THE SUCCESS CONTINUUM

FOS can strike at any point on the Success Continuum, depending on your history and ability to tolerate the feelings associated with striving for and achieving success.

As you study your FOS pattern, observe where on the Success Continuum you self-sabotage. Where do you tend to go off track?

- In the beginning stage when you are preparing to achieve and enter the gate?
- When you're just out of the gate and beginning to make progress?
- After you achieve a small measure of success?
- After you achieve moderate success?
- When you are solidly in the success zone?
- After you reach the top of the success zone and are about to catapult into the zenith of your career?
- When you are at top of your field consistently?

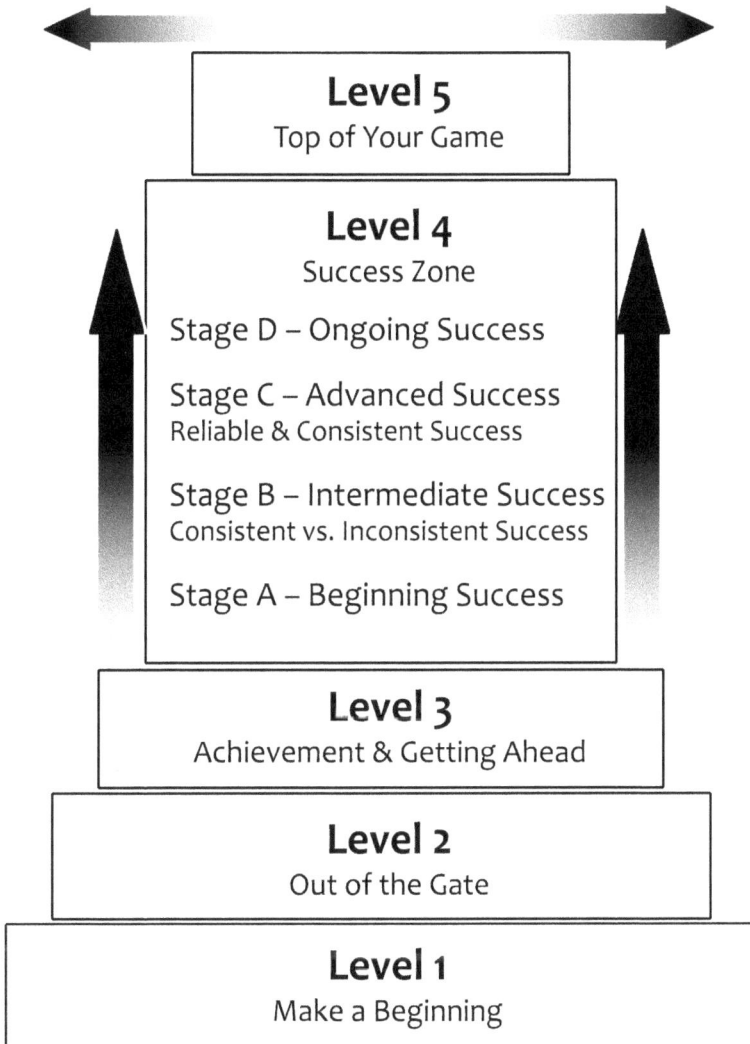

CHART YOUR ACHIEVEMENT PATTERNS

Create two graphs, label one My School Achievement Graph and the other My Work Achievement Graph, in order to graph your achievement history. On the left side of the graph list the Success Continuum:

Top of the Game
Success Zone
     • Stage D
     • Stage C
     • Stage B
     • Stage A
Achievement/Getting Ahead
Out of the Gate
Beginning

Across the bottom identify the timing of your achievements.

Years 1–5
Years 5–10
Years 10–15
Years 15–20
Years 20–30
30+

Put a dot on the graph illustrating where you were on the Success Continuum each year in your school or work history. Then connect the dots. The result should look something like graph on the following page.

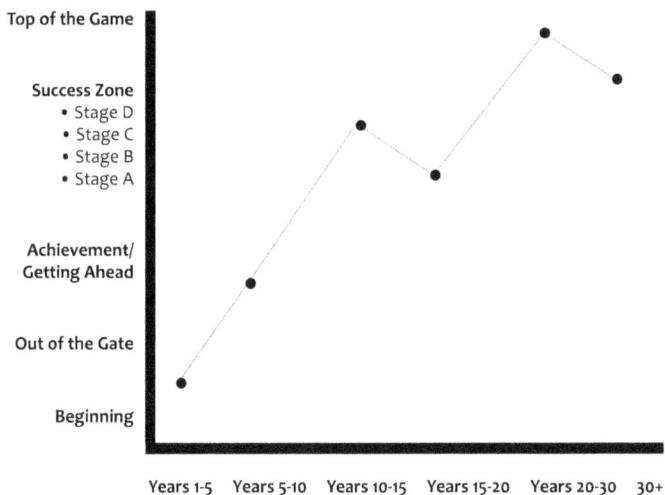

Top of the Game

Success Zone
- Stage D
- Stage C
- Stage B
- Stage A

Achievement/
Getting Ahead

Out of the Gate

Beginning

Years 1-5   Years 5-10   Years 10-15   Years 15-20   Years 20-30   30+

USING THE INFORMATION

These graphs are powerful illustrations of our achievement history. Look for clues about your FOS Signals in the times when your success has faltered. Document what you learn about yourself through these exercises and share with your Success Buddy (see Chapter 11: Tool 1). The insights are valuable catalysts for awareness.

CHAPTER 3

FEAR OF SUCCESS PERSONALITY TRAITS, PATTERNS & SYMPTOMS

FOS is an equal opportunity troublemaker. It doesn't care about your age, gender, race, nationality, cultural orientation, or socioeconomic status. People with FOS can be found in every industry and at every stage on the Success Continuum.

The FOS personality has:

- Innate gifts that manifest as an intense interest or passion to take creative action;
- A strong desire to use these gifts and share them with others;
- A strong desire to succeed;
- The talent and ability to reach their personal best.

These personality traits operate in the FOS scenario:

1. Vacillating self-esteem;
2. Fear of criticism and disapproval;
3. Fear of failure, *which is not a main driver of FOS*, but does play a small role;

4. Fear of people feeling angry, jealous, or getting competitive when one achieves success;

5. Ambivalence toward success, producing opposing desires: a strong desire to succeed; and a desire to back away from success when one gets close to the goal.

The Personality Traits Up Close

VACILLATING SELF-ESTEEM

Vacillating self-esteem has a negative effect on performance and productivity. A self-esteem issue is characterized by feelings of inadequacy, insecurity and unworthiness. The result is self-doubt and a lack of confidence in one's ability to succeed.

Vacillating self-esteem refers to feeling confident about oneself one minute and "not enough" the next. Vacillating esteem is characterized by paradoxes, such as feeling:

- Worthy and unworthy
- Better than and less than
- Adequate and inadequate
- Secure and insecure
- Connected and disconnected

Healthy self-esteem produces feelings of confidence, empowerment and a desire to connect with others. In contrast, bruised self-esteem produces feelings of self-doubt and a desire to isolate from others. Bruised self-esteem most often represents a long-standing issue with oneself that can be traced back to childhood or adolescence.

Take the case of Rebecca who started to doubt herself and engage in self-sabotage.

Rebecca

Rebecca, a sophomore in high school, came to me depressed and upset about her low grades. An assessment of her elementary and middle-school performance revealed a roller coaster history of academic achievement.

By the end of 8th grade, Rebecca's parents were worried she would not get into a good college. The three agreed on a plan for high school that included maintaining high grades and getting active in extracurricular activities. Hoping to motivate her into high performance, Rebecca's parents offered her financial incentives for high achievement.

During her freshman year, Rebecca attained high grades in all her classes, was active with the school newspaper and student government and played in the orchestra. She made new friends and had a strong social life. Academically successful, socially popular and happy with her extracurricular activities, Rebecca spent less time at home.

In the second half of her freshman year, her parents began to complain about her schedule. Upset she wasn't home for family dinners, they expressed concern and worry about her "packed" schedule. They suggested she was overloading herself and asked questions like "Are you sure you can handle all this?"

At first, Rebecca dismissed her parents' concerns. She was confident about her schoolwork and extracurricular schedule. Little by little their concerns "wore her down." She began to experience self-doubt and insecurity. When she vocalized her conflict, her mother said, "Not everyone is good at multitasking."

Despite her growing conflict, Rebecca finished her freshman year successfully. The aftereffects came in her sophomore year. Her grades dipped. She felt overwhelmed by her schedule. No matter how hard she tried, she couldn't get back on track. She described it as a "slump." She was experiencing FOS.

At the beginning of our work, she did not connect her performance issues to her parents. I challenged her on this and slowly she began to connect the dots. She realized that her parents had been giving her contradictory messages about achievement for many years. She recalled instances when her parents encouraged her to do something and then complained when she did it. She remembered feeling confused by their contradictory communications, which she interpreted to mean "we want you to succeed" and "we don't want you to succeed."

As our work progressed, Rebecca became aware that her parents had given her a double message about achievement all her life. She remembered being five years old and memorizing words to a long song. Proud of herself, she sang it to her parents. After she was finished, her mother complimented her and then asked, "Did it hurt your head to memorize all those words?"

She remembered feeling deflated, angry and scared and defiantly told her mother, "No—it didn't hurt my head. I'm going to memorize more long songs." But she never did.

In therapy, we concluded those early childhood experiences planted the seeds for the FOS pattern that emerged as academic and social underachievement. While she overcame that pattern her freshman year, it surfaced full force in her sophomore year.

Rebecca's story illustrates that the messages we receive in our formative years leave lasting impressions. They count, and they take up residence in both our conscious and unconscious mind.

These messages get acted on and follow us into our adulthood if they are not addressed. When we receive clear messages of support, we act autonomously and move in the direction of our goals. Contradictory messages cause self-doubt and mature into limiting beliefs and FOS symptoms.

FEAR OF CRITICISM AND DISAPPROVAL

Individuals with FOS have a fear of criticism and disapproval. Why? In early childhood and/or adolescence, criticism and disapproval deflated us and chipped away at our self-esteem.

Fear carries a very specific message. It tells us we will not get something we want; we will lose something we have; or we will get something we do not want such as rejection, humiliation or abandonment.

Fear causes anxiety and anxiety plays a prominent role in the FOS scenario. Anxiety is deeply intertwined with FOS because there is a strong fear of disapproval and criticism, anticipation of negative outcomes and concern for how one is perceived.

Anxiety is a problem. It takes a toll on you to feel it on a consistent basis. Its psychic message says, "Be careful, you are not safe." It reminds you that the more visible you are, the more likely you are to experience disapproval. If you heed that message, you will hold back in fear or find some other way to deal with the danger you feel. Some people overcompensate and forge forward in the face of fear. Others hide or try to keep a low profile while being visible.

The funny thing is this: even though people with FOS experience mild to severe anxiety on an ongoing basis, they are unaware they are experiencing anxiety. Don't let this happen for you.

To become aware of your anxiety level, learn how to take your anxiety temperature. It's an easy way to measure how much anxiety you're feeling at any moment. Chapter 15: Tool 5 will show you how. Just follow the directions in the section, "Take Your Anxiety Temperature", and you'll have a simple, handy way to track this bothersome emotion.

You may discover you are more anxious than you realized and that you have ignored or medicated your anxiety with activity, distractions, or addiction to work. There are better ways to handle anxiety. Chapter 15: Tool 5 has tips and suggestions for that. You can lower your anxiety. For now, be aware that anxiety might be playing a role in your life. See if you relate to Mitzy.

MITZY

Mitzy, a successful editor, was unaware anxiety was running her life. She had trouble sleeping and reported she would get up in the middle of the night and work. She would constantly think of stories and ways to get authors involved in writing pieces for her publication. Her explanation was, "I love what I do, and I have to keep on top of everything. I'm in a very competitive arena." Once she took her anxiety temperature, she discovered she had an emotional baseline of moderate to high anxiety. I asked her how she experienced her anxiety before our work and she said, "I thought I was a perfectionist and being hyper-creative. But now that I'm tuning into my anxiety temperature, I realize that I'm worried and fearful, a lot."

If you're like Mitzy, you may be mislabeling or ignoring this important emotion. One way to lower anxiety is to become aware of the role fear plays in your life. Fear drives anxiety. To lower and eventually eliminate anxiety you need to face your fears and immunize yourself (not numb yourself) against them. This means developing new and efficient coping strategies for dealing with your fear of criticism, disapproval and the pressures that come along with visibility and success. The toolkit section suggests ways to handle these issues.

FEAR OF FAILURE

Fear of failure plays a small part in the FOS drama, but it is not the main driver. However, fear of failure does show up in the FOS scenario as self-doubt and limiting beliefs that say, "You may fail" or "This won't work." While this makes the FOS individual feel unsteady and insecure, the threat of failure is not overriding.

In addition, fear of failure produces a different profile and achievement history than FOS. Individuals with fear of failure as their predominant problem are not in the competitive arena and do not demonstrate a strong desire to strive for success. Their achievement history is flat rather than up and down like those with FOS. And lastly, the individuals with fear of failure do not have a history of being identified as talented with the potential to succeed and do not have a track record of going for it.

FEAR OF PEOPLE FEELING ANGRY, JEALOUS, ENVIOUS OR COMPETITIVE

Those with FOS are sensitive to what others feel and intuitively take the emotional temperature of those around them. This happens automatically, on an unconscious level. While success looks desirable from a distance, up close it can be difficult to handle. FOSers get nervous when people feel jealous, angry, envious or competitive with their success.

FOSers are especially sensitive to "toxic envy." Melanie Klein (1975) calls "toxic envy" a very specific kind of envy where people "feel angry that another person possesses and enjoys something desirable," and they have an "envious impulse to take it away or to spoil it."

For some of us, knowing someone wants to take what we have or re-place us is scary and unnerving. It conjures visions of an experience that may not be survivable.

People with toxic envy often act out, causing irreversible damage. This is especially nerve wracking to those with FOS.

The problem with toxic behavior has become painfully clear as social media gains a more prominent position in our lives. Over the last few years, suicides and depression have increased as privacy rights have been violated. Today, technology allows "haters" to broadcast to hundreds, thousands and millions of people in a nanosecond.

Feeling unsafe bodes badly for a person with FOS who not only thrives on approval and positive feedback, but would ideally like a one hundred percent approval rating. While that is unrealistic, it is also exhausting and fruitless to place one's resources and energies into a goal that can never be reached.

The solution is simple but not easy. FOSers must develop an immunity to toxic envy, anger, jealousy and the competitive feelings of others. They must also learn new strategies and coping skills to deal with these emotional states and give up their need to achieve a one hundred percent approval rating.

AMBIVALENCE TOWARD SUCCESS

The fifth FOS personality trait has to do with a deep sense of ambivalence toward success. This is characterized by a strong desire to succeed and a desire to back away from success.

When positive and negative feelings coexist, ambivalence develops. Therefore, individuals with FOS have two minds about success. Success is attractive and success is scary. The conscious mind sees success as positive and the unconscious mind regards success as unsafe and dangerous.

On the surface, success seems like a good thing. It's socially acceptable and is a rewarding outcome of passion and hard work. On the other hand, success comes with a price tag. You lose anonymity and are more closely scrutinized. You're more prone to vacillate between grandiosity and depression. There is a tendency to get drunk on the high of success.

The contradictions cause ambivalence. The ambivalence produces a pattern of moving toward success with great energy and then backing away from success by acting out on symptoms like procrastination, holding back in fear and performing inconsistently. While success has the potential to reward us financially and give us status, fame, power and special privileges, it also causes pain, discomfort, disappointment and conflict. Let's take a closer look at how ambivalence operates.

FOS PATTERNS

What drives the FOS pattern is an unconscious fear and ambivalence toward success. The fear stands side-by-side with a strong desire to achieve and strive for a goal. This motivates the FOS personality to move toward his or her goal. When he or she gets within a certain proximity to success, fear kicks in. When that happens, the unconscious comes to the rescue and compels the individual to engage in self-sabotaging behaviors that move him or her away from the goal.

Exactly where this happens on the Success Continuum depends on your childhood and adolescent experiences. Think about the questions below and see if you can trace the origins of FOS in your life. To help jog your memory, take a look at your school and work achievement graphs. They should reveal a pattern of FOS behavior.

Answer the following questions to get a better understanding of your own ambivalence:

1. How were your accomplishments handled in your family when you were a child or adolescent? Did you receive conflicting messages about success, i.e., it is okay to succeed and that it is not okay to succeed?
2. How did your peers react to your achievements?
3. How did teachers and significant authority figures treat your accomplishments?
4. How did your parents respond when you acted independently?
5. How did significant caregivers and other important people in your life (parents, extended family or friends) respond to your successes or your creativity?
6. What level of safety did you feel when you were being genuine and vulnerable?
7. Did you trust that others would help you get what you want?

The FOS Behavior Pattern for Inconsistent Performers

1. A history of up and down performance despite having the skill, talent, or creativity to achieve consistently;
2. A tendency to start out strong and pursue success diligently while you are moderately distant from both success and failure;
3. A tendency to stay committed to the goal and to work with increasing energy if success is in sight but still fairly distant;
4. A tendency to become anxious and show signs of ambivalence as you reach one of the following points on the Success Continuum:
   - The cusp of success
   - A measure of success

- The success zones
- The top of your game

5. A tendency to sabotage your success by doing one or more of the following:
   - Engaging in behaviors that will interfere with or derail your momentum
   - Devaluing your achievement
   - Behaving in ways that create distance from your success

6. A tendency to regroup as one moves away from the success zone and toward the failure region, and then begin again to pursue success in a vigorous and focused way to regain the goal or a substitute for it.

The FOS Behavior Pattern for Sabotage at the Top

1. A history of achievement that often can be traced from childhood or adolescence into adulthood.
2. A strong desire to achieve and the ability to work diligently toward a goal; reaching for short- and long-term successes.
3. A tendency to experience self-doubt or a lack of confidence despite a history of success.
4. An ability to be productive for sustained periods of time and then, seemingly out of the blue, engage in self-destructive behavior that interferes with or derails success without regard to the position, reputation or status achieved.
5. A fall from grace as self-sabotage derails career success.

PART II

Manifestations of Fear of Success

CHAPTER 4

Vision Issues

Are You Doing What You Love?

When you love what you do and feel engaged in your work, you feel involved and connected to what you are doing. Work feels meaningful and you feel you are doing the work you are meant to do. You're fulfilling your purpose.

Unfortunately, an overwhelming majority of us do not feel engaged in our work. Studies of American workers found that less than thirty percent feel engaged in their work. A study of the work force in 142 countries revealed that only thirteen percent of workers feel involved and connected to what they do.

Addressing this work crisis, Schwartz and Porath (2014), wrote "Why You Hate Work", concluding that, "For most of us . . . work is a depleting, dispiriting experience, and in some obvious ways, it's getting worse."

If you are a member of the depleted, dispirited group, make a change. Understanding and facing why you're unhappy can help you pinpoint your Vision problem. Focus on resolving the blocks that interfere with being engaged at work.

These questions might help:

- Am I doing my right livelihood?
- Does my work environment inspire me to do my best work? If yes, how? If no, why not?
- Does my work bring me joy?
- Does my work feel fulfilling and meaningful?

This chapter can open your mind to the possibility that you can tune into your passion, convert your passion into work you love and create a career that flows naturally from your innate talent.

I believe Vision work is vital to creating a career that gives you an opportunity to use your natural abilities and share your gift with others. Most importantly, Vision work awakens the passion that is already inside you and moves you in the direction of doing what you love and following your bliss.

Following Your Bliss

The phrase "follow your bliss" was used by Joseph Campbell in 1985 while videotaping a series of conversations with journalist Bill Moyers. The talks were edited into a documentary, *The Power of Myth*, that aired on PBS in 1988, a few months after Campbell's death. In one segment (Episode 4), Campbell said:

"If you do follow your bliss you put yourself on a kind of track that has been there all the while, waiting for you, and the life that you ought to be living is the one you are living. When you can see that, you begin to meet people who are in the field of your bliss, and they open the doors to you. I say, follow your bliss and don't be afraid, and doors will open where you didn't know they were going to be . . . doors will open for you that wouldn't have opened for anyone else."

When asked by Moyers if there is a price for not following your bliss, Campbell quoted the last line from Sinclair Lewis' novel, *Babbitt* (1922), when George Babbitt says, "I have never done a thing in my whole life I wanted to do."

This vignette illustrates that the consequence for not doing what you want to do is deep regret and personal loss.

After the program aired on PBS, the term "follow your bliss," become popular and an everyday part of the American lexicon. Nowadays, Campbell's phrase has gone global. People all over the world are interested in living in their potential and following their bliss.

Leaders promoting self-actualization encourage us to aspire to our personal best. Marianne Williamson promotes the concept through her talks on *The Course in Miracles*. Deepak Chopra and Oprah Winfrey offer a series of 21-day meditations to help you tune into your best self. Sharon Salzberg's books, *Real Happiness* (2010) and *Real Love* (2018) proposes that meditation helps you tune into your highest self. And, Brene'Brown advises everyone to muster their courage to be their authentic self and do what they are meant to do.

Even commercials promote self-actualization. AARP advertises, using the theme, "Live in the possibilities." A car company uses the tagline, "Dare Greatly." The concept "follow your bliss," encompasses phrases such as: "Live Up to Your Potential;" "Do What You Love;" "Dare to be you;" and "Follow Your Passion."

Find Your Calling

Each of us finds our calling at different moments in time. Some early, some later. Among those who find their calling later in life, there is a group that tuned into their passion early and were discouraged from following their bliss. These individuals slowly turned their focus to other endeavors and gave up doing what they loved. Their passion, repressed, resurfaced in later years.

It's never too early or too late to find your calling.

Some get there early. At three years old, Pablo Picasso followed his mother around the house saying "*piz, piz,*" (the short form for pencil in Spanish). As soon as she gave him a pencil, he started drawing. By five, he was producing full figures. Michael Phelps, the Olympic gold medal-winner, started swimming at seven and set a national record in the 100-meter butterfly three years later. At two and a half, on his own initiative, hockey player Wayne Gretsky, picked up a hockey stick and began practicing for hours at a time in his grandmother's living room.

Others found their destiny later in life. Colonel Harland Sanders, the creator of the Kentucky Fried Chicken franchises, became a business mogul at age 65. Laura Ingalls Wilder published her first book, *Little House in the Big Woods,* at 65, and went on to pen seven more that were known as the *Little House on the Prairie* series. The TV show based on the books ran from 1974 to 1983. Anna Mary Robertson Moses, better known as Grandma Moses, famous for American folk-art painting, didn't pick up a brush until she was 76. She went on to paint for over twenty more years and lived to see her work sell for more than $10,000 a canvas. She died in 1961 at age 101. In 2006, her painting, *Sugaring Off,* sold for US $1.2 million.

While I'm no Picasso, I did find my calling early. By three, I was keenly focused on what people were feeling. I am told that by age four I was giving unsolicited advice (which I often do today, even though I know better) to my parents, their friends and anyone else who would listen.

I was only five and a half when I started helping the kids in my neighborhood solve the problems they were having with their parents, siblings, teachers and friends. That experience set me on the path of doing what I love. By nine years old, I knew I would be a therapist.

My career is an outgrowth of my passion and a desire to resolve psychological problems and resistances to success. This surfaced for me in the early years and I do now what I did then. Today, of course, I'm formally trained, educated and experienced. I have a larger toolkit than I did at five and a half, but my passion is the same. I love what I do today as much as I did all those decades ago.

How's Your Passion and Vision?

Not knowing your passion and not having a Vision is a problem that prevents you from flourishing in your work life. It also has a negative impact on your soul and your self-esteem. You survive, rather than thrive in your career and creative endeavors. This will bring you to the painful realization that you are not living up to your potential.

A Vision issue is no fun and is usually accompanied by *false news*. It lures you into believing that identifying your passion, doing what you love and following your bliss is impossible. The false news makes it difficult to take constructive action toward your goals because you feel discouraged, depressed and hopeless.

These powerful feelings trigger self-sabotage and, before you can blink an eye, FOS is in motion interrupting momentum and making trouble. Procrastination, a common form of sabotage, slows down the action to a snail's pace. In a worst-case scenario, you feel too overwhelmed to take action at all. A psychological paralysis sets in and all constructive action stops. There is a solution, but first you must identify and clarify your Vision issue.

Assess Your Vision

Clarify your Vision issue by taking the Vision Issue Checklist below. Then read about the different types of Vision problems in the section that follows and identify your problem further.

VISION ISSUE CHECKLIST

Check each statement that applies to you, even if it applies only part of the time.

❑   I cannot tune into my passion.
❑   I question whether I really have a passion.

❑   I have a clear Vision but can only manifest part of it.
❑   I don't know how to convert my passion into my right livelihood.
❑   I feel my Vision is too big and that prevents me from making a beginning.
❑   I am waiting for my Vision to magically emerge or appear.
❑   I do not recall ever knowing what I loved to do.
❑   I know what I love to do, but I have trouble earning a comfortable living doing it.
❑   I question whether I can earn an abundant income doing what I love.
❑   I never had a dream or Vision.
❑   I had a clear dream but gave up on it.
❑   I have multiple talents and interests and find it difficult to choose one career path.
❑   I feel afraid to take a risk and commit to my Vision, because I might fail or discover it's not my Vision after all.
❑   I followed someone else's Vision for me instead of finding my own.
❑   I am searching for my spiritual and creative self.

VISION ISSUE TYPES

What type of visionary are you? Read the descriptions below and identify how you would describe yourself.

CLUELESS VISIONARY

1.   I cannot tune into my passion.
2.   I don't know how to turn my passion into creative action.
3.   When I get in touch with my passion, it slips away.
4.   I have difficulty creating a Vision and I think:

- I don't know my passion, and I never did.
- I don't know what I want to do.
- I don't have a creative goal.

Overwhelmed Visionary

- I have a Vision, but it feels too big and this prevents me from making a beginning.
- I feel afraid of my Vision.
- I cannot make a beginning.
- I have created a support system to help me, but I still feel overwhelmed and have trouble taking action.

Inconsistent Visionary

- I have a clear Vision and know what I love to do, but I work on my Vision inconsistently.
- I take two steps forward and one step back.
- I am stuck in Stage B on the Success Continuum.
- I engage in FOS signals that stop me from moving through Stages C and D on the Success Continuum.

Defeated Visionary

- I have given up on my dream because I've been told my Vision is unrealistic, ridiculous or stupid.
- I am influenced by the negativity of others.
- I have a harsh Inner Critic that negates positive feedback from myself and others.
- I sometimes feel determined to go for it, but I slip back into hopelessness and despair.

Beware

Vision problems can keep you stuck for long periods of time. Days, weeks, months and even years pass when creativity slows to a crawl or comes to a complete stop. When everything stops, you have entered the despair zone.

It's crucial to recognize the early warning signs of falling into despair. Early on is the time to take constructive action to reverse negative thinking and hopelessness.

In the Toolkit section, you'll learn how to recognize and address despair before it takes up residence in your psyche. If you feel despair now, please talk to someone about it, as soon as possible. Action is the antidote to depression and despair. To get started, get support to take at least one action a day. No matter how small the action is, taking action on a reliable and consistent basis will help lift your depression and move you out of the despair zone.

CREATING A CAREER VISION

To create a career Vision, you need to tune into your passion and allow your passion to lead you to doing what you love.

I am not alone when I tell you people are happiest when their work reflects their passion. This state of happiness comes from engaging in their right livelihood, which emerges from inside you and reflects the mission you are intended to fulfill while you are here. This is your purpose and your divine gift to others.

PASSION

As we gain mastery over our environment, passion emerges naturally. It shows up in childhood and adolescence as a keen interest or fascination in a particular activity. When you think about things that grabbed your attention in your early years, you will see they were connected to your passion.

Where does passion come from? I believe it is built into our spiritual and psychic DNA. We come into this world with innate passion. Our likes and dislikes manifest from the beginning. We are born with personalities, predispositions and preferences.

As a child, there were things you liked and the things you didn't.

Ransack your memory and you will find example after example of things that captured your interest and attention. There were activities you loved and activities that bored you. Some things caught your interest, while others you ignored. Your likes and dislikes aren't random. They have a common denominator: an underlying pattern you can trace to your innate passion.

Therefore, passion arises naturally from within our natures. No matter how hard we try to ignore or suppress it, passion will find a way to get our attention.

CONNECT TO YOUR PASSION

Tuning into your passion is easy for some, difficult for others and a huge challenge for most people. A good many of us have been taught to dismiss our passion. Some have buried it so deeply in the unconscious that it seems as if it was never there at all.

Being disconnected from our passion, no matter what the cause, leaves us adrift, much like a boat without a navigation system. It's hard to head for a destination if you don't know where you want to go.

The good news is this: passion never dies. It may get repressed or suppressed. It may seem dead, but it's not. It's merely dormant, patiently waiting for an opportunity to make itself known.

Passion is patient, persistent and resilient. It will try to get your attention by emerging as a fleeting idea, daydream, or desire to do a specific kind of work. It may even present itself as a vision others label "unrealistic." Nevertheless, it does appear, letting you know it's still alive.

I believe we are meant to use our natural talents to engage in work that gives us meaning and purpose. When our passion is imprisoned, it is hard to find our right livelihood and feel fulfilled. Work without meaning or doing a job you hate, leads to feeling unhappy and discontented with your work life. Your inner language may sound like this:

- "I don't feel good about what I do."
- "My work has no meaning or purpose."

- "I feel bored and unfulfilled at my job."
- "I don't like what I'm doing, but I don't know what I want to do."
- "I wish I knew my passion, but I don't."
- "People talk about passion and 'following your bliss,' but I'm not sure that's realistic."
- "I think I want to do _____ (fill in the blank), but I don't trust that's really what I want to do."
- "I can't remember ever having a passion."

Problems Can Develop Early

Conflict about one's passion often develops in early childhood or adolescence. Somewhere along the developmental scale, a significant person—family member, nanny, teacher or peer—ignored, dismissed or diminished your passion. Clinical research shows that passion is sensitive in the early years. For most children and adolescents, it's difficult to hold onto passion in the face of being ignored, teased, ridiculed, criticized, disparaged or overly corrected for it.

Passion needs support to blossom and flourish. If you're having trouble tuning into your passion or dedicating yourself to helping it flourish, you can be sure *you did not receive the encouragement and support you needed to honor and hold on to your passion*. If you have a problem with this as an adult, your passion was significantly suppressed or repressed in your early years.

The good news, as I said earlier, is that passion never dies. While others may have influenced you to repress, suppress or ignore your passion, they did not succeed at killing it. Passion is hardy. It refuses to be pushed aside or remain invisible forever. It lies dormant inside you, waiting patiently for a chance to emerge.

Passion persistently nags until you pay attention. It looks for opportunities to communicate with you. While you're sleeping, passion communicates through your dreams. During the day, it will make you feel uncomfortable about your work life. It appears spontaneously as a vision, daydream or creative idea. When it gets tired of being buried in your unconscious, it gets in your face, so you have to pay attention.

The in-your-face method reminds me of a scene from the TV series, *Family Guy*. (MacFarlane, Zuckerman, 1999–2017) In one scene, little Stewie tries to get his mother's attention. She ignores him. Determined to get a response from her, he calls her name repeatedly, saying, "Mom, mom, mom, mommy, mommy, mommy, mum, mum, mum." He continues until she shouts, "*WHAT?*" He smiles demurely and says "Hi!"

While the scene hits our funny bone (check it out on YouTube), it illustrates a more serious message: persistence works! Like Stewie, your passion will demand you acknowledge its existence, and it will persist until you do.

Vision work can help you get in touch with your passion and give it permission to emerge and flourish.

VISION WORK

Vision work is the work we do to tune into our passion, turn our passion into creative action, and turn our creativity into work we love.

When passion is prevented from evolving naturally, it needs a nudge to rise to the surface. Vision work gives passion this nudge.

Gather your best courage and fortitude and move forward. Vision work requires commitment, faith, persistence and support. Here's where your Success Buddy or Success Group can be helpful. Each will accompany you on the journey to self-actualization.

Doing Vision work is like digging for oil or searching for lost ships at sea; it is painstaking work that pays enormous dividends. The ultimate goal of Vision work is to earn your living doing what you love.

I call the work you love, your **A-Job**. If you cannot earn a comfortable living from your A-Job, get a **B-Job.** A B-Job utilizes your talents, pays the bills, gives you benefits and is in a convenient, comfortable environment. The B-Job will give you peace of mind and financial relief while you make a plan to do your A-Job on a full-time or part-time basis. Later in the book (Chapter 19: Tool 9: Create an Action Plan, and Chapter 21: Tool 11: Get Your Financial Life on Track), I'll say more about the A-Job and B-Job.

Passion Doesn't Always Garner Support

Even when passion emerges early, it isn't always met with environmental support. The Austrian poet Rainer Maria Rilke said he knew he was a writer at a young age because he "had to write." His parents did not support his poetic nature. Hoping to dissuade him from a career as a poet, they sent him to a military academy in a city south of Vienna. Fortunately for the world, Rilke's intense passion won out. He rejected military life and became a world-renowned poet and philosopher. His views on writing and life are memorialized in the letters he wrote to family, friends and colleagues.

One set of extraordinary letters is captured in a small volume titled, *Letters to a Young Poet*, published in 1929 by Franz Xavier Kappus. It is a collection of ten letters that passed between Kappus and Rilke from 1902 to 1908.

The first letter, from Kappus to Rilke, was written in 1902 when Kappus was a 19-year-old cadet at Rilke's former military academy. Kappus was confused about whether to pursue a military career that offered financial security or pursue a career as a writer, riddled with financial uncertainty. Kappus, inspired by Rilke's commitment to become a poet and his success, wrote to Rilke asking for advice.

Kappus wanted Rilke to critique one of his poems and tell him if he had the talent to become a poet. Instead of commenting on the quality of Kappus' poems, Rilke advised Kappus how to find his own answers. He advised him to turn inward (do the Inside Job) for the answer. It's an eloquent and wonderful description of how to tune into your passion and dedicate yourself to your Vision:

> "You ask whether your verses are any good. You ask me. You have asked others before this. You send them to magazines. You compare them with other poems, and you are upset when certain editors reject your work. Now (since you have said you want my advice) I beg you to stop doing that sort of thing. You are looking

52

outside, and that is what you should most avoid right now. No one can advise or help you—no one. There is only one thing you should do. Go into yourself. Find out the reason that commands you to write; see whether it has spread its roots into the very depths of your heart; confess to yourself whether you would have to die if you were forbidden to write. This most of all: ask yourself in the most silent hour of your night: must I write? Dig into yourself for a deep answer. And if this answer rings out in assent, if you meet this solemn question with a strong, simple "I must," then build your life in accordance with this necessity; your whole life, even into its humblest and most indifferent hour, must become a sign and witness to this impulse."

Rilke, Rainer Maria
February 17, 1903
(Rilke, Kappus, 1929)

Despite the ambivalence Kappus expressed to Rilke about pursuing a military career, he did complete his military training and served as an officer in the Austro-Hungarian army for fifteen years. It was a financial decision. A writer at heart, Kappus did work as a newspaper editor and journalist after he retired from the military. He also wrote poetry, humorous sketches, short stories and novels. In addition, he adapted several works (including his own) into screenplays for films in the 1930s.

In the language of *Success Is An Inside Job®*, Kappus' military career was his B-Job. It provided him with financial security. But he didn't abandon his writing. He continued to write while serving as an officer. After he retired, he pursued his A-Job (writing) full-time. As Rilke advised, he resolved the question, "Must I write?" by tuning into his strong desire to do so. While he resolved his conflict differently than Rilke, he did find a way to do what he loved. He did achieve success as both a writer and military officer.

Rilke's sincere and heartfelt prescription for life—tune into your passion and follow your bliss—influenced Kappus deeply. We can all benefit from Rilke's wise counsel.

Vision is About Following Your Bliss

The Inside Job is about living your best life and self-actualizing. To do that, you must move in the direction of your Vision and your bliss. This is simple, but not always easy. In the toolkit section, we will focus on these steps:

Five Steps to Doing What You Love

1. Tune into your passion.
2. Convert your innate talents, skills and abilities into activities you love.
3. Create your right livelihood from doing activities you love.
4. Earn your living from your **A-Job** or move in that direction with a **B-Job**.
5. Share your gifts with others by doing work that is meaningful to you.

If you do work you feel emotionally, spiritually and intellectually invested in, you will feel happy and content. Our planet needs you to tune into your passion, do what you love and follow your bliss.

*   *   *

The Inside Job gives you the opportunity to live in your potential and use your natural gifts to create your right livelihood. We are all built for greatness. Begin to release yours now.

When you tune into your passion, you begin to do the work you are meant to do. You will feel inspired and joyful on a daily basis. Take my experience as an example. Today, I feel as excited and inspired to help others as I did at five and a half.

I know for sure if you tune into your passion and inner vision you will discover your right livelihood. Some of you reading this right now will invent new products and services. Others will become activists or politicians, artists, athletes, business or computer experts, educators, farmers, musicians, entertainers or performing artists, plumbers or electricians.

The possibilities are endless. You will contribute to our planet by building houses and skyscrapers. You will focus on climate control and install solar panels. You will farm, dig wells, do expert plumbing. You will start schools, revise educational systems. You will help the abused, the handicapped and downtrodden. You will counter injustices. And some of you will help others get out of their own way, as I do.

Whatever your calling, your gifts will manifest in your work, every day. They do for me, and they will for you.

CHAPTER 5

UNDEREARNING

"Many of us have deep spiritual and psychological patterns around money that can block our efforts at managing our money better and creating prosperity."

Mari Geasair
Writer-Educator

THE UNDEREARNING SYNDROME

A common symptom of FOS is underearning. Underearning is characterized by earning less than you deserve given your talent, ability, expertise and experience.

Underearning causes emotional discomfort and financial insecurity. Underearners are in a constant battle between their income and expenses. The majority of underearners have an income history that falls into one of these scenarios: 1) income is not sufficient to meet monthly/yearly expenses; or 2) income covers the primary expenses with little, if any, money left over.

With the exception of the Affluent Underearner (see the definition below), most underearners find it difficult to build reserve funds, save or plan for their older years.

As a group, underearners tend to be hard workers who have a strong desire to establish financial security. Despite this goal, underearners struggle. This is true across the job spectrum.

My experience suggests four types of underearners:

- **The Struggling Underearner**
  The struggling underearner survives rather than thrives, constantly battling to meet basic expenses. Many underearners live paycheck to paycheck and have no health insurance. Most have no reserve funds for emergencies and little or no savings.
- **The Surviving Underearner**
  The surviving underearner has enough income to just get by. There is enough money to cover basic expenses, healthcare, a small amount for entertainment, and some luxury items. Usually there is a very small reserve fund for emergencies, but often no college fund, and meager savings and retirement accounts.
- **The Debtor Underearner**
  The debtor underearner supplements income by borrowing money from family, friends, credit cards, and banks. He or she may sell personal assets such as property, stocks, bonds, jewelry and art, or liquidate savings accounts or pension plans. This may help short-term but is unsustainable long-term because it depletes equity. These solutions do not solve the underearning problem. They always add more stress and worry to an already difficult financial picture. By accumulating debt or depleting assets, the debtor underearner creates a two-fold stressful financial problem—underearning and debt.
- **The Affluent Underearner**
  Affluent underearners earn well but still struggle financially. For a number of reasons, they may agree to work for a fee or income that does not match their level of experience or expertise. They often overspend or live above their means. Acting out on FOS Signals, they get fired or are forced to

resign due to personality conflicts, antisocial interactions, a clash with the organization's culture or an inability to collaborate or cooperate.

There Is A Solution

Underearners, especially those struggling and in debt, often feel shame, which makes the situation worse. Know that you're not alone, and you don't have to "fix this" alone. Underearning is reversible. Digging out of the hole requires determination, persistence and action. Most importantly, it requires patience and a positive support system. Seek help and, if needed, professional advice. Suggestions are listed in the resource chapter. The good news is that if you take the right action on a consistent basis, you can overcome underearning. First things first: make a beginning. Follow the tips below:

Tips for Struggling, Surviving and Debtor Underearners

1. Work with your Success Buddy to establish what type of underearner you are. It's possible you're a mixture of two or three.
2. Get help.
3. Stop debting and/or overspending *immediately.*
4. Create a spending plan. Put yourself and your family on a budget and stick to it.
5. Get solvent:
   a. Get your income to match your minimum expenses (housing costs, utilities, food, clothing, and transportation). This may mean changing jobs or adding a second income to your earnings.
   b. Stop increasing your debt, one day at a time.
   c. Work from a personal or business spending plan (if you have a small or medium business).

TIPS FOR AFFLUENT UNDEREARNERS

1. Work with your Success Buddy and clarify your issue.
2. Identify your assets and the FOS Signals contributing to your self-sabotage.
3. Ask for a raise or change to a job that pays a salary commensurate with your track record, experience and expertise.
4. Stop overspending and work from a spending plan.
5. Downsize your lifestyle if necessary.

START ABUNDANCE AND PROSPERITY THINKING

Think abundantly and prosperously. Abundance and prosperity are Vision-based thinking. Underearning thinking leans toward the negative with worrying characterized by thoughts such as, "There will never be enough," or "We may lose everything!"

Prosperity thinking is based on positive beliefs about the future and affirmative thoughts about yourself.

Underearning problems leave you feeling fearful, despairing, and hopeless. Surviving becomes a way of life. Unhealthy financial practices become habitual and without knowing it, underearners normalize the abnormal. Stop! You deserve better. Use the tools in Chapter 21: Tool 11: Get Your Financial Life on Track and dedicate yourself to changing your circumstances.

CHAPTER 6

UNDERACHIEVING

Being gifted does not guarantee that you will actualize your gifts. While knowing you are gifted is good, acknowledging your gifts is better. Using your gifts is best. Underachievers don't use their gifts fully.

The word "underachiever" was first used to describe students who performed below their grade level or academic abilities. The word "underachievement" became associated with a discrepancy between a child or adolescent's school performance and his or her actual ability. Now, we use the word "underachiever" to describe any individual, group or team that has the talent, skill or ability to perform, but is not living up to his/her/its potential.

While there are many variables that contribute to the underachieving syndrome in adults, we can glean knowledge from research on gifted students. It is estimated that less than ten percent of all identified gifted and talented children and adolescents self-actualize and use their gifts as adults.

Joan Franklin Smutney (2004) identified the main causes of underachievement in gifted children:

1. Lack of motivation to apply themselves.
2. Environments that do not nurture their gifts and may even discourage high achievement.
3. Difficulties or other learning deficits that mask their giftedness.

JR Whitmore (1980) found the following to be the leading characteristics of underachieving gifted students:

1. Low self-esteem.
2. Consistently negative attitude toward school and learning.
3. Reluctance to take risks or apply oneself.
4. Discomfort with competition.
5. Lack of perseverance.
6. Lack of goal-directed behavior.
7. Social isolation.
8. Weaknesses in skill areas and organization.
9. Disruptiveness in class and resistance to class activities.

The characteristics that contribute to underachieving in school-age children and adolescents set the stage for FOS. Low self-esteem, the reluctance to take risks, lack of perseverance and disruptiveness all interfere with internal motivation and goal-oriented behavior. These traits manifest in adulthood as FOS and FOS Signals such as bruised self-esteem, self-criticism, fear of taking risks and competition, a tendency to get distracted by people or secondary projects, problems with aggression, and an inability to stay focused on a goal.

Since the majority of identified gifted children and adolescents grow into underachieving adults, it's not surprising they display the following FOS symptoms: underperforming, performing inconsistently, or cycling in and out of performing at their personal best.

It's estimated that about ninety percent of the students identified as gifted during their school years do not use their gifts as adults. Current statistics exclude the large number of students whose talents remain unidentified, either because the schools don't assess the category or the gifts are masked. Therefore, my theory that we are all born with innate gifts that can be cultivated has not been sufficiently tested.

As a former teacher who has worked with thousands of children and adolescents over the course of my career, I can say with some assurance that there are vast numbers of school-aged kids whose talents go unrecognized.

Many are above average at abstract thinking, creative problem-solving, leadership, sales, entrepreneurial endeavors, and psychosocial dynamics and strategies.

While schools readily identify students with gifts in sports, reading, writing, science and math, and music, dance, or art, they aren't in a position to assess the talents of students with gifts outside these typical categories.

Are Underachievers Aware of Their Problem?

Some of us are aware we are underachieving because we are unhappy and restless. Since innate talent and passion never dies, our gifts nudge and nag us. As a result, some of us stay in touch with our unrealized potential and others give up and feel no motivation to use their gifts and talents.

A friend told me a story about her brother Frank, a classic underachiever. Frank works in the mailroom of a big company. He's always on time and never takes sick days. The company recognizes his potential, and every year at his review his bosses beg him to accept promotions or take advantage of the company's one hundred percent tuition reimbursement program. Every year, Frank categorically refuses: "I'm not interested in any of that." A look at his childhood tells us he was a very bright boy born left-handed with a hearing problem and dyslexia. Not hearing well, not reading well, and forced by his teachers to write with his right hand, Frank was belittled by his parents, siblings and teachers. Neither his hearing loss nor dyslexia was addressed, and both interfered with his school achievement. This bright man was taught to thoroughly fear success. To date, he shows no interest in changing.

Chronic underachieving is downright depressing. You feel stuck and discouraged. The mental and emotional stress can cause physical symptoms such as exhaustion, neck and back pain, headaches, stomach problems, and more. The emotional discomfort can surface as mood swings, anxiety, depression, hopelessness and even suicidal thoughts.

This is difficult to conquer alone. If you are physically or emotionally depleted due to FOS, do something about it now. Start by working with a Success Buddy. Add a consult with a professional trained in resolving chronic FOS issues.

You are not alone. Many underachievers have a classic push-pull dynamic with success. They want to use their talents and skills for optimal performance and creativity but are hampered by FOS Signals such as inertia, procrastination, distraction, negative self-talk and perfectionism. These FOS Signals cause inconsistent performance and lack of confidence.

Others, like Frank, become apathetic. They cannot or will not acknowledge their talents and gifts. They no longer have any interest in pursuing a goal or motivation to nurture their potential. They are resigned to just survive, not thrive! If you are like Frank, I want to say, "It doesn't have to be like this. There is a solution. Give yourself a gift and begin the process. See where it takes you. I think you'll be so much happier and enjoy a more meaningful life."

Types of Underachievers

There are three types of underachievers: the knowledgeable underachiever; the confused underachiever; and the unconscious underachiever.

THE KNOWLEDGEABLE UNDERACHIEVER

Knowledgeable underachievers are somewhat sophisticated and conscious of their problem. They have showcased their gifts and have achieved a certain level of competence and success in their field.

They have established identities as gifted, talented or skilled people. They tend to be passionate, intense and unafraid to unleash their talents. Despite self-doubt and harsh Inner Criticism, they have an established track record of using their talents. However, when they get to a certain level of performance, they slide backward and have to climb back again, just as in the game of Chutes and Ladders. Some even feel they are "clawing" their way back again.

THE CONFUSED UNDERACHIEVER

Confused underachievers are baffled by their up-and-down track records. They often do not understand why they have performance issues, why they have times when they're on a roll and why there are times they're stuck. During periods of low performance, they resemble an athlete in a slump. They know they are underperforming but can't dig themselves out of the deep hole they're in.

THE UNCONSCIOUS UNDERACHIEVER

Unconscious underachievers have given up on their talent and themselves. They work at jobs below their levels of talent and are often unaware of their underachievement. Internal motivation and ambition are either low or nonexistent. Unconscious underachievers are sleepwalking through their work life and see no other alternative.

If you are the partner, a family member or friend of an unconscious underachiever, see if you can help this person wake up. Look for someone who was in the same position and has solved the problem. If the unconscious underachiever can get in touch with his or her potential and get support to bring some of this talent to the surface, the process can begin.

*   *   *

Are you unhappy and not clear why? Do you have gifts but aren't sure why you can't access them fully? Make a beginning. The Inside Job will help lower the frequency and intensity of underachieving periods. Begin by leaning on your Success Buddy and support system. Make a commitment to use your talents reliably and consistently. The fourteen tools in the Toolkit section will help you with the process.

Try. It can pay off!

CHAPTER 7

WORKAHOLISM

Workaholism is an addiction to work. It's characterized by these symptoms:

- You predominantly live to work and think mostly about work.
- You engage with your work to the exclusion of other activities.
- Your work takes precedence over family, personal relationships, relaxation and play.
- Your life becomes emotionally, spiritually and physically imbalanced.

Workaholics actually enjoy these symptoms, preferring work to the exclusion of everything else.

THE WORKAHOLIC CHECKLIST

Check the statements that apply. If you can say "yes" to three or more of these statements, you may be a workaholic.

- ❏ I take work home with me consistently.
- ❏ I work during weekends and vacations.

- ❏ I talk about work more than any other subject.
- ❏ I like work more than any other activity.
- ❏ I work more than forty hours a week.
- ❏ My attitude and actions give others the impression that sleep, relaxation and play are all a waste of time to me.
- ❏ I feel happiest when I'm working.
- ❏ I find myself thinking about how to solve work-related issues during my time off.
- ❏ My family and friends have given up on expecting me to be on time.
- ❏ I am energetic and competitive at work, but at home I often feel lethargic and depressed.
- ❏ My sense of personal value and esteem is connected to my career.
- ❏ My ability to set boundaries and have a sense of control is most stable in the work environment.

Workaholics lead unbalanced lives. According to Bryan E. Robinson, author of *Chained to the Desk: A Guidebook for Workaholics, Their Partners and Children, and the Clinicians Who Treat Them,* (1988) workaholics have few friends, few or no hobbies, do not take care of themselves and derive their esteem from the work environment.

Juliet B. Schor, an economist, researched work hours in the United States and found that Americans now work 200 hours a year more than they did in 1970. In work hours, this equals an extra month of work.

In her book, *The Overworked American: The Unexpected Decline of Leisure,* Schor (1991) posits that working longer hours is not necessarily bad. It brings rewards like promotions, salary increases, bonus points with the boss, and deriving satisfaction from your accomplishments. It's only when work eclipses other areas of your life that it's time to stop and rethink how you are living.

TRY THIS

You can learn the most from paying attention to how you feel when you're away from work. Robinson recommends rating your satisfaction with family life, friendships, health and hobbies on a scale of one to five, one being the least satisfied and five being the most satisfied. Remember to add your points up correctly. If your total is fewer than 10 points, it might be time to cut back on work.

How Do You Become a Workaholic?

Children of parents with emotional problems are often put on the path to workaholism when they become responsible for their siblings, house-work and parents. In families where the parent-child roles are reversed, the child or adolescent takes on various responsibilities of the parent. We call these kids "parentalized" children. If you grew up as a parentalized child or adolescent, your self-esteem was built, in part, by being in charge and making sure things got done. Parentalized children are self-motivated and are used to creating structure so the family doesn't fall apart. Children taking on these roles, take on full-time jobs. They sacrifice a certain portion (if not all) of their childhoods and adolescence.

We also find parentalized children in families where the parents are not present, whether because of their addictions, emotional dysfunction or physical disabilities. These families produce kids who learn that it's much easier to focus on tasks than to deal with the painful feelings brought about by their family lives. This kind of avoidance is most often carried into adulthood. In Robinson's book, he describes what he did to cope with his father's death. Robinson was in college when his father died. He became obsessed with finishing three big papers rather than dealing with his grief.

Robinson's research and clinical experience shows that workaholism is closely correlated with an inability to be intimate. I concur with his findings: many of my workaholic clients enter treatment because their close relationships are at risk or falling apart.

Regardless of what kind of home you grew up in, if you're a workaholic you display certain personality traits. Rigidity and perfectionism are at the top of the list. If you have been a natural achiever all your life, or what we call a "born" achiever, you are likely to become a workaholic.

Signs of Workaholism

We see early warning signs of workaholism in childhood or adolescence by observing how kids approach studying, sports or other interest areas. Those with a tendency toward perfectionism or anxiety about the quality of their performance, and those who need to receive approval through achievement are at risk for adult workaholism. Those who were talented, but did not achieve much in their early years, may also be at risk because they have something to prove to themselves and the world.

Adding to the problem is the fact that most work environments reward workaholism. These work cultures refer to workaholics as dedicated, hard workers who exceed expectations. Young adults who have displayed workaholic behavior or who have latent tendencies can easily metamorphosize into full-fledged workaholics at their jobs.

After almost two decades of research, Robinson has identified three different categories of workaholics:

1. The All-or-Nothing Workaholic
2. The Relentless Workaholic
3. The Savoring Workaholic

THE ALL-OR-NOTHING WORKAHOLIC

The All-or-Nothing Workaholics do things perfectly or not at all. They struggle to get started on projects for fear of not meeting their own impossible expectations. When they do get rolling, they binge to the point of exhaustion. Low self-esteem leads those who suffer from this style to worry compulsively about work, while blaming themselves constantly for not doing it.

THE RELENTLESS WORKAHOLIC

These types don't have problems getting started; it's the stopping they have trouble with. They can't say "no," set priorities or delegate responsibilities. They often work so quickly that they make careless mistakes.

THE SAVORING WORKAHOLIC

The Savoring Workaholic obsesses over details to the point of paralysis. These individuals hate letting projects go and will often create additional work when the task gets close to completion. Robinson found a perfectionist aspect to "hanging on to the project" that involves what I call narcissistic or grandiose thinking:

- "No one can do it as well as I can."
- "If I don't do it, it won't be done right."
- "It won't have my mark."

WORKAHOLICS DON'T PLAY WELL WITH OTHERS

Workaholics of all stripes are generally terrible team players, says Gayle Porter, a professor of management at Rutgers University. "They try to control other people and information. They allow crisis situations to develop because it makes them look like a hero." The result is that workaholics are often not getting much accomplished. That's why Porter thinks more bosses would do well to reward those who clock out at the end of the day. "The employee who wants to go home is the one who will be most efficient during the week, because she's protecting her time off." (Goodman, 2006)

WORKAHOLISM AND FEAR OF SUCCESS

When we study how workaholism operates, it is easy to understand why it represents another manifestation of FOS. Porter's research shows that workaholics are underperformers and have a great need to come across as heroes. This need to fix and control people, projects, and outcomes underlies the workaholic personality and encompasses many of the characteristics of FOS personalities, such as bruised self-esteem from early childhood and adolescence; the need to gain approval and avoid disapproval from self and others; and a strong desire to avoid painful feelings and intimacy.

OTHER RESEARCH ON WORKAHOLISM

Clark, Leichook, and Taylor (2010) give us more insights into the workaholic personality. For example, perfectionism and narcissism are highly correlated with workaholism, as are other personality traits:

- Emotional instability.
- Impatience, which conflicts with conscientiousness and the compulsion to work.
- An ability to multitask, having several events occurring simultaneously: referred to as the "polychronic control" component of workaholism.

TIPS FOR REINING IN YOUR WORKAHOLISM

Use Tools 7 and 9 (Chapter 17: Tool 7: Clarify Your Vision; Chapter 19: Tool 9: Create an Action Plan) to create an Action Plan to address workaholism. Here are a few tips:

- **Shut down your cellphone, laptop and electronic screens.** Leave your cellphone in the office and eat lunch out of the office. Do not take your laptop, cellphone or tablet to bed or to the dining room table. Reduce checking e-mail on weekends.
- **Learn to prioritize.** Learn what work tasks are important and what can be handled later.
- **Practice a "First Things First" philosophy.** Take care of yourself better and practice putting relationships and relaxation first. It's a way to recognize that some things in life are more important than others.
- **Get a handle on your To-Do list.** Set a cutoff for the number of tasks that can reasonably be accomplished in a day: no more than five. If a new task must be added, knock another off that demands equivalent time. And schedule time for play.

ADDITIONAL SUGGESTIONS

To get the most from the tips above, I recommend keeping a journal of your reactions and feelings to cutting back on your workaholic behaviors. As with any addiction, you can expect to experience some form of withdrawal. Pay special attention to feelings, thoughts and behaviors that come up when you are not working. Record when you feel anxious or irritable.

Also write about any behaviors that serve as a substitute for workaholism. We call this "addiction substitution." These include excessive use of substances (alcohol, drugs, food) or activities (sports, sex, surfing the internet, reading, watching television, gardening, or home improvement projects) to fill in the time you previously devoted to work.

WHEN WORKAHOLISM GETS OUT OF HAND

When a workaholic goes from functional to dysfunctional, everyone knows it. Co-workers, superiors, subordinates, family and friends, even casual acquaintances can see clearly when a workaholic has crossed the line.

When workaholics derail, they cause havoc. These circumstances sometimes call for immediate action, even a forced resignation.

If you are a workaholic heading for dysfunction, your best option is to catch the problem in time, take a leave of absence and begin a program of recovery.

Loving what you do and feeling complete satisfaction from work is a wonderful gift to yourself and others. It taps your creativity and gives you an opportunity to put your natural talents and abilities to work. Dedication to work need not be a problem if your life includes intimacy, relaxation time and fun activities with family, friends and acquaintances. Work is only a problem when it's out of balance with the rest of your life.

CHAPTER 8

Sabotage at the Top

We Are All at Risk for Sabotage at the Top

Only a small percentage of people reach the top of their game and stay there. Performing reliably and consistently at your personal best is a challenge, and relatively few people stay at the top for years. This accomplishment is so rare that we follow the careers of these successful and unusual people with great interest. Actresses Meryl Streep and Judi Dench, business magnate Warren Buffet, and entrepreneur Oprah Winfrey are examples of such remarkable performers. What gives these extraordinary people the ability to achieve at such rarified levels for so many years? What personality traits contribute to the longevity of their success?

While the answers are complex and unique to each individual, they do share a number of personality traits, attitudes, and behaviors. People who perform at their peak over time:

- Are passionate about what they are doing and have a Vision.
- Love what they do, care deeply about their work and are talented at it.
- Stay humble, grateful and emotionally centered.

- Keep their focus on their Vision and use courage, risk-taking and determination to achieve their goals.
- Are hard workers who are ambitious, resilient, persistent, and creative.
- Listen to their inner voice and intuition.
- Follow the adage, "Never, never, never, give up."

WHAT IS SABOTAGE AT THE TOP?

When you engage in behaviors that have the potential to seriously interfere with or derail your career, that's Sabotage at the Top. These behaviors may start out innocuously, but over time the frequency and intensity increase until they endanger your work or creative endeavors.

PSYCHOLOGICAL DYNAMICS

Some of the emotional components driving Sabotage at the Top are:

- Feeling insecure.
- Being self-critical.
- Feeling grandiose, arrogant or overly powerful.
- Behaving in a demanding, aggressive or condescending manner.
- Minimizing or denying feelings of fear, pressure, stress or anxiety.
- Letting others talk you out of addressing feelings of discomfort.
- Acknowledging feeling fear, pressure, or stress, but thinking *I'll deal with this later, when*:
  a. Things calm down.
  b. I have some downtime to address them.
  c. I have time to figure this out.
  d. I can take a vacation.

76

Behavioral Patterns that Endanger Your Performance

Why do people self-destruct after they reach the pinnacle of their performance or after a big win? What triggers high performers to derail—and are there early warning signs?

Of course, each individual's personality and psychosocial history is different. In my experience, people who engage in Sabotage at the Top resemble the great figures of Greek tragedy and classic tragic heroes or heroines who slipped into states of ambition, pride, overconfidence, self-doubt or self-sacrifice, which eventually led to their downfall.

Looking at Sabotage at the Top from a different vantage point, many who fall find it difficult to handle the pressures of success with humility and gratitude. They find it difficult to stay centered and "right-sized," which causes them to engage in FOS behaviors that interfere with their creative gifts. Little by little, the FOS Signals begin to chip away at high performance, productivity and self-confidence. They put obstacles in the path of new projects. They over-perform or "dial it down." A downward spiral begins to emerge, and then our modern tragic figures slip into grandiosity or depression.

THE GRANDIOSITY PATTERN

Star performers often feel good about visibility and success, but after the initial glow, they tend to go through these five stages:

STAGE 1: **The arrogance of success.** They slip into grandiosity and overconfidence about their success.

STAGE 2: **The pursuit of more.** They slowly slip into over-indulgence characterized by overspending, demanding and expecting special favors, collecting an entourage, engaging in addictive behaviors (drugs, alcohol, food, sex, inappropriate relationships, shopping) and feeling better than others.

STAGE 3: **Denial**. They are unwilling to acknowledge there is a problem or that Stages 1 or 2 put them at risk or in jeopardy.

STAGE 4: **Fear**. They realize they are sabotaging their success and they begin grasping for a solution. This approach can work if the individual addresses the problem before they completely derail.

STAGE 5: **Derailing**. They face the truth that they have been in denial and acted self-destructively, derailing their hard-earned success.

Behaviors associated with arrogance and grandiosity are abuse of alcohol, drugs, food, or sex; gambling; compulsive computer use; inappropriate sexual activities (acting out sexually, sexual harassment, extramarital affairs, romantic obsessions, engaging with escorts or prostitutes); over- or under-using power or leadership skills; inappropriate handling of money; workaholism; or engaging in high-risk activities.

THE DEPRESSION PATTERN

Most top performers who slip into the depressive pattern feel good, at first, about their success. Some do not. Those who initially bask in the glow of their achievement experience success as an antidote to bruised self-esteem and self-doubt. For others, it is another story. They do not credit their success to their talent or hard work. Quite the opposite. After the initial glow, their mood spirals downward through:

STAGE 1: **Confusion and self-doubt**. Instead of feeling good about their success, negative feelings, such as anxiety, fear and self-criticism, rise to the surface despite positive feedback from others.

STAGE 2: **Engaging in overindulgence or deprivation to medicate and counteract depressed feelings**. They feel a strong desire to isolate and withdraw to protect themselves when not working. Many cannot identify they feel depressed.

STAGE 3: **Denial**. They deny that they have a problem or are at risk or jeopardy from Stages 1 and 2.

STAGE 4: **Grasping for a solution**. They acknowledge something is wrong and grasp for a solution. If they seek help from a professional experienced in and trained to resolve sabotage at the top, they can recover from the depressive pattern. If not, they slip into Stage 5.

STAGE 5: **Surrender to the truth that they are too depressed to perform optimally or that their careers have derailed**.

A WORD TO HIGH PERFORMERS, ENTREPRENEURS, CEOS AND SENIOR LEADERS

Without realizing it, high performers, entrepreneurs, CEOs, and senior leaders can cause themselves, their companies or their teams to self-destruct. When individual high performers slip into a grandiose or depressive pattern, they are at risk for Sabotage at the Top. Therefore, the Inside Job approach works across industry lines for the C-suite in business, entrepreneurs, sports teams, and organizations, as well as for individuals.

Sabotage at the Top is such a powerful pattern, it can cause organizations to decline. In his book, *How the Mighty Fall*, James C. Collins (2009) and his team reveal how companies with outstanding track records derail. Their research focused on a few significant questions:

- Can decline be detected early and avoided?
- How far can a company fall before the path toward doom becomes inevitable and unshakeable?
- How can companies reverse course?

Collins' research shows that decline happens in five stages and that it can be avoided, detected and reversed. These are the stages:

STAGE 1: Hubris (Arrogance) Born of Success
STAGE 2: Undisciplined Pursuit of More

STAGE 3: Denial of Risk and Peril

STAGE 4: Grasping for Salvation

STAGE 5: Capitulation to Irrelevance or Death

Explaining the stages, Collins says that decline begins when a company's leader or leaders slip into a state of arrogance. They lose sight of what brought about the company's success. They feel overly confident about the company's performance, and their sense of superiority creates a false sense of security.

According to Collins' research, when in Stage 1, the company has a track record of success and is in the profit zone, usually holding cash assets. Success goes to the head of CEOs and their senior leaders. They get over-confident and slip into a grandiose state. As they do, they begin to act out Stage 2, the Undisciplined Pursuit of More. They make decisions to expand their operations or buy other companies. Little by little, the company stops doing what it did to be successful and then leaders slip into Stage 3, Denial of Risk or Peril. Rather than pause, take a breath and assess, they keep moving forward, expanding their operation from the inside or buying companies to multiply their holdings.

Collins found that *denial* is a key component to derailing. He explained how:

> "Our principal effort focused on a two-part question: What happened leading up to the point at which decline became visible, and what did the company do once it began to fall? . . . Our comparative and historical analysis yielded a descriptive model of how the mighty fall that consists of five stages that proceed in sequence. And here's the really scary part: You do not visibly fall until Stage 4! Companies can be well into Stage 3 decline and still look and feel great yet be right on the cusp of a huge fall. Decline can sneak up on you, and—seemingly all of a sudden—you're in big trouble."

Despite the overwhelming evidence that leaders of highly successful companies can slip into egotistical states of overconfidence and grandiosity that pushes them off the original game plan that produced success, Collins is confident that can be avoided:

> ". . . I ultimately see this as a work of well-founded hope. With a road map to decline in hand, institutions heading downhill might be able to apply the brakes early and reverse course. We've found companies that recovered—in some cases, coming back even stronger—after having crashed down into the depths of Stage 4. Our research indicates that the organizational decline is largely self-inflicted, and recovery largely within our own control. So long as you never fall all the way to Stage 5, you can rebuild."

What Can We Learn from
How the Mighty Fall?

Individuals, like companies that slip into grandiosity and begin to derail, can look and feel good while on the decline. Sabotage at the Top begins when success triggers arrogance or depression, the pursuit of more and the denial of risk or peril.

These three stages cloak reality. It's like playing Russian roulette with your success. We have seen celebrities, politicians, sports figures, trust-fund babies, and prominent businesspeople fall. For some, success proved fatal. The list is long: Diane Arbus, American photographer; actors Keith Ledger and Philip Seymore Hoffman; Michael Jackson and Whitney Houston; fashion designer Alexander McQueen; and Lembit Oil, the Estonian Chess Grandmaster. All were all brought down by success and unresolved FOS issues.

To me, Collins' most important finding is encapsulated in this quote:

> "Organizational decline is largely self-inflicted, and recovery largely within our own control . . . as long as you never fall all the way to Stage 5 . . . ."

Like companies that decline, individuals can avoid complete derailment, as long as Sabotage at the Top is detected early and reversed.

TAKE PRECAUTIONS

If you are exhibiting symptoms of Sabotage at the Top, begin to address the problem immediately. Invite someone to be your Success Buddy. Watch for red flags: feeling depressed; a dip in mood; wanting to isolate; feeling grandiose or a bit overconfident. Beware of getting "high" off success; being overly impressed with the attention and the "pack" you belong to; getting addicted to special treatment; beginning to numb out with alcohol, drugs, food, money or sex; feeling you are above the rules; collecting an adoring entourage; making unreasonable demands; or denying you're in trouble.

Heed those red flags. Return to a more centered and focused place. How?

- Stay humble and "right-sized."
- When you feel yourself slipping into grandiosity or depression, get support. Go back to your roots: remember who you are and how you got where you are.
- Keep the slogan "Less is more" in the forefront of your thinking. Do not engage in the undisciplined pursuit of more.

HOW TO PRACTICE LESS IS MORE

- Do not become overly invested in accumulating more of anything, including material possessions, projects, an expanded entourage, or false friends.
- Stay connected to people who have your best interest in mind.
- Create an "Inner Circle" of four or five people you trust.
- Nurture your spirituality.
- Talk with your Success Buddy.
- Form a Success Group that gives you honest feedback. If you trust them, they will point out if you're in denial about sliding into grandiosity and depression.

- Honor your gifts. Remember the only reason you're successful is because you are using your talent creatively and sharing it with others. You're making the planet a better place. You can't do that if you feel depressed or grandiose.
- Protect your private time and balance it with time for family and friends. If you're in the public eye, take time to do some community service or philanthropic work.
- Imitate those in your profession who handle themselves and their success well.

CHAPTER 9

More Ways Fear of Success Affects Us

FOS can manifest in myriad ways. While the main psychological driver is the same (unconscious fear), FOS is ingenious and resourceful and can appear in many forms. Earlier we showed how it drives Vision issues, underearning, underachieving, workaholism and Sabotage at the Top. In this chapter, we look at other ways FOS can interfere in your work life.

Here are some additional manifestations of FOS:

- Inconsistent performance.
- Difficulty making a career change or transition.
- Feeling unhappy despite financial success.
- Shutting down possibilities of doing what you love.
- Difficulty navigating corporate waters.
- Difficulty meeting entrepreneurial goals.
- Difficulty in your current situation, despite loving what you do.

Inconsistent Performance

A common form of FOS is inconsistent performance, characterized by periods of high performance (being "on fire") and low or poor performance. In terms of doing one's job, it can manifest in a variety of ways and patterns.

Some people perform for months at a time at an efficient and creative pace and then fall into a period of low performance. Others can only work efficiently and use their talents for part of a day or a week.

Inconsistent performance can cause up-and-down earnings. While inconsistent performance is problematic at all times, it is a critical problem for those whose earnings are closely linked to performance. This is true in entrepreneurial endeavors, sales, finance (investment banking, wealth management, trading), and real estate, where inconsistent performance swiftly threatens job security and earning power.

In addition, certain professions are completely dependent on reliable and consistent performance, such as sports, the fine and performing arts, and writing. Artists and writers must produce so they have something to sell.

Even those whose earnings are not so closely bound to performance should keep in mind that performance and success are linked, no matter what. Inconsistent performance hurts your career and takes a toll on your self-esteem. It shakes faith in yourself and fosters insecurity. Intuitively, you know you have more potential, but can't stabilize your performance. This is frustrating! No matter what you do, you are stuck. Vacillating between high performance and low performance keeps you from being successful. Take action early to reverse this. Tools 12 and 13 (Chapter 22: Tool 12: Prevent Sabotage at the Top; Chapter 23: Tool 13: Safeguard Your Success) can help you heighten your awareness and identify red flags.

Difficulty Making a Career Change or Transition

Your heart will let you know if you need to change your career. Maybe you're thinking of a transition to a new role or position, or of moving to a new company, organization or city. Feeling discontent, pain, or being downright miserable alerts you that something is wrong. Whether or not you know what you want to do next, one thing is for sure: where you are now is not reflecting your bliss.

FOS prevents us from facing the truth and creating a plan to move forward. Are you in that position now? Are you holding back in fear and not facing your situation head-on because the change you want to make seems daunting or too difficult? If your answer is "Yes" I want you to know that change is not only possible, it is highly recommended. With the right encouragement and support, it is doable. Is it easy? No. Can it be done? Of course!

Take Carlos, for example, who decided to make a career change at age forty-eight. Carlos had an exciting and satisfying career as a competitive dancer. He held titles in the top three tiers for more than fifteen years. After he retired, he opened a premier dance studio, which became a family business, employing his mother, father and siblings. He taught dance to recreational and competitive dancers for another fifteen years.

He came into treatment to address his growing discontent with managing the studio and teaching dance. As a result of our work, he decided to sell the studio and train to be a therapist and psychodrama coach. He completed his master's degree in psychoanalysis, and then decided to do a second master's in social work to broaden his work options. Today, he works in an out-patient treatment clinic with clients in early recovery from substance abuse and has a private practice. He loves his work. Carlos' story can be your story.

To heighten your awareness and clarify your problem, ponder these questions:

- Do I love my field?
- Is my dream job in this field or industry?
- Can I get what I want from my current situation, or do I need to move to another role, organization, or city?

Feeling Unhappy Despite Financial Success

Working at a job where the main reward is money is emotionally and spiritually depleting. If you are stuck in a job that is financially rewarding but feels meaningless, make a plan to change. Do the Vision work to start tuning into your passion and discovering what you love to do. Create a wish list for how you want to live the next chapter of your life. You may need to save money before you make a move, or use some of your savings to bridge you through your next steps.

Shutting Down Possibilities of Doing What You Love

If you're ignoring potential opportunities for doing what you love, your bliss will keep nudging you. A persistent feeling of unrest will nag you. Your inner voice will whisper, "I'm capable of more than this!"

My friend Monique knew for many years that she should be doing something else. We met in April 2013 and discussed our work histories. She said she was a writer. I told her I was writing a book about resolving career blocks and FOS issues. Once I described FOS, she said she knew she had it and was holding herself back from becoming a screenwriter.

Monique was born in Paris to French parents who moved the family to the United States when she was eight. Missing Paris, Monique returned for college and never left. When I met her, she was 35 and had a well-established life in Paris. She frequently visited friends in the US, but her main social and business connections were in Paris.

She earned a small living by writing screenplay and commercial treatments and helping her boyfriend sell real estate in Paris. Although they had a lovely apartment and life together, Monique shut down her career possibilities for a very long time.

A breakthrough came for both of us after one of her visits to New York.

She agreed to give me feedback on this book. I emailed her what I had at the time. She didn't respond for a couple of months. I finally emailed her, saying I wouldn't feel destroyed if she didn't like the book; I genuinely wanted her opinion, and it wouldn't keep me from completing the book.

Here's what she told me:

> "I am so sorry I haven't gotten back to you on the book. I love it. I didn't just read it; I *did* the book and it's changed my life. I've known for over ten years I should be in LA writing screenplays, but I didn't have the nerve to do it. I've been procrastinating and denying the truth. I read all about FOS and did the exercises. I overcame my inertia and Francois and I are moving to LA in January. We're engaged and will get married before we arrive so he can get a green card and work legally in the US."

I was blown away. Not everyone has such an immediate response to doing the work. It does show how quickly FOS can be leveled if you're ready and willing. Today, Monique is a working writer. In the last four years, she's totally changed her life. She co-wrote a play that was performed in Mexico City to rave reviews. They're making it into a full-length film. She's written two TV pilots, worked as a screenplay doctor and is now a full-time script reader for a film production company. She is writing another TV pilot with her former mentor who is now her co-writer. Monique is on her way less than five years after deciding to overcome her FOS.

Difficulty Navigating Corporate Waters

It's not always easy to fathom corporate cultures and gain recognition for your expertise, experience and ability to contribute to the company.

This problem may be that you are under- or overusing your strengths. Reread the FOS Signals Checklist to see what FOS behaviors are sabotaging your success. Then embark on a mission to practice new behaviors and learn new coping skills. You can turn this situation around, but you have to work at it, patiently and consistently.

Difficulty Meeting Entrepreneurial Goals

Being an entrepreneur is hard work. Entrepreneurs are often the sole creators, founders and drivers of the business. You are Renaissance men and women who are able to multitask and run many aspects of the business. And therein lies the risk. Having too much on your plate can become overwhelming. For some, not being able or willing to delegate tasks can sabotage your ability to do what you do best.

The same prescription applies here as for those who have difficulty navigating corporate waters. Go over the FOS Signals Checklist and see what behaviors are sabotaging you. Get a Success Buddy and create a tight supportive Inner Circle. The world needs what you are creating. Don't get stuck. Get the support you need to thrive.

Difficulty at Work Despite Loving What You Do

Even if you love what you do, FOS can make trouble. See if you relate to any of these statements:

- I love what I do, but:
  a. I've been passed over for a promotion or raise.
  b. I resist taking a position of leadership, although I have years of experience and the expertise required.
  c. I find it difficult to speak at meetings. I avoid taking a position on issues because I'm afraid of people's anger, criticism, negative judgment, or passive-aggressive behavior.
  d. I have social anxiety and it dampens my ability to interact fully with others.
  e. I'm financially successful but feel unfulfilled.

If you love your job or role and the field or industry you are in, try to resolve your FOS problem in your current position and stay where you are. Use the Success Is An Inside Job® Toolkit to develop an Action Plan that addresses your specific situation. You have a problem that can very well be solved where you are.

If you love what you do but find the role or the work environment unsuitable to your personality or sensibility, think about changing jobs. First, assess if a move is really necessary. If it is, decide what kind of move you want to make. Do you imagine you'll be happy making a horizontal move or is a vertical move your desire? A horizontal move is lateral; it does not come with a new title, salary or bonus. You'd move to a different boss, division, or team, with your salary and benefits remaining the same. A horizontal move can improve your morale, work conditions and the quality of your creative input. The move increases your happiness but not your salary or status.

A vertical move is up or down. Moving down by choice can be positive if you want less responsibility and you're in a financial position to take a pay cut. Moving down involuntarily usually means you've been demoted in responsibility and status. Moving down involuntarily is not good. It shows there's been a breakdown between you and your company, between you and your Vision, or both.

It can be scary acknowledging you're unhappy or mismatched to your job. It entails acknowledging you no longer love what you do or admitting you never were doing your right livelihood. Then you have to do the work required to find your right livelihood.

Ultimately, you'll need to face the fact that you have to make a change, or even transition to a totally different career. While this phase of your career development may not be a walk in the park, it is doable. Just muster your courage and develop the willingness to retool, reschool, and reinvent yourself in service of doing what you love.

Of course, you must discover what you love before you embark. This means clarifying your Vision.

Transitioning to another career may feel like rolling a huge rock up a steep hill, but I assure you, it's worth it. The hours and years you waste feeling unhappy should be proof that the easier, softer way is to make a change. This is the better way.

Ruben's case illustrates that changing careers is possible at any age, even if you are transitioning from a career you have loved.

Ruben

Ruben's father and uncles worked in the garment industry. At twenty, Ruben quit college and followed suit. At first, he sold textiles. Eventually, he transitioned to color and style forecasting and opened a boutique firm.

The business had up-and-down earnings and was moderately successful for thirty years. Ruben underearned for the entire life of his business but loved the lifestyle. He stood shoulder to shoulder with designers from top clothing manufacturers. He made good friends. He went to runway shows and shopped Europe for his clients four or five times a year. Whether he made money or not, Ruben was happy for a while.

However, struggling in business is not fun. Ruben was worn down from being an underearner and underachiever. Periodically, he got into a financial rut and needed to be bailed out by family and friends. Like all good survivors, Ruben continued doing business and living in New York City, armed with his dogged persistence and very low rent from a rent-controlled apartment.

The problem: Ruben was not prosperous, often in debt and had no financial backup, savings or retirement account.

Fortunately, Ruben had another innate gift. He loves, and is good at, listening to problems, giving advice and helping people recover from addictions. Over the years, many people suggested he become a therapist.

However, the idea of transitioning to another career seemed daunting to Ruben. He had no confidence he could get through college to earn a B.A., let alone the master's degree he would need. He arrived at our Success Is An Inside Job® workshop in a panic about closing his company and finding another way to make a living.

"What am I going to do now? I'm almost 66. I have no savings, no pension, and no financial security."

At the workshop, Ruben did Vision work, creative brainstorming and research. With guidance from the facilitators and his Success Buddy, Ruben created an Action Plan. His first task was to secure money to pay his basic expenses. He was eligible and took Social Security. That gave him a small income and medical benefits. Second, he found a college that accepted his former college credits, gave college credits for business experience, helped him secure age-based scholarship money and student loans, as well as a job through the college's work-study program.

He went back to school at sixty-seven and graduated at seventy-one with a B.A. in psychology and social work. This enabled him to enroll in a masters of social work program. To fund graduate school, Ruben applied for and won a scholarship, took out student loans and used his Social Security to stay afloat.

During the SIIJ workshop, he created a Vision and mission statement that read: *My vision is to use my MSW to do organizational consulting. My mission is to resolve resistances to success and fear of success issues in the fashion industry.*

Ruben completed his M.A. and is now an employed social worker. Today, at age seventy-three, he works full-time for an organization that serves clients recovering from substance abuse. He feels appreciated and loves being a therapist. In the future, he plans to split his time between organizational work, private practice and consulting.

Ruben's case illustrates that you're never too young or too old to create a Vision and mission and to *go for it*. All things are possible if you are determined and garner the right support such as your Success Buddy, Success Group and Inner Circle.

There's a Solution for Every FOS Scenario

Some of you are in a job that meets your financial needs, but you're not doing what you love. Others are stuck in unhealthy work patterns and jobs that feel unfulfilling.

If you're asking yourself, "Is this all there is?" the answer is "No." There is more, but you have to do some soul searching and Vision work to find it.

If you are having trouble navigating corporate waters and are not getting ahead in your present culture, take a look at your FOS Signals list and see where you're in your own way. Again, a Success Buddy can be invaluable to your process. You might need to change how you interact with people or learn new skills to be successful in your present culture. Make sure this is where you want to make your mark. If you are doing work you love (or really like), you might also invest in an executive coach who has experience and expertise in your field.

My hope for you is that you open yourself to discovering your right livelihood. This requires being receptive and accepting of your intuitive thoughts and spontaneous insights. While it can feel overwhelming and intimidating to begin the journey of self-discovery, it can also feel exciting. The reward is incredibly worthwhile and life changing. It is so much more fun to do work you love than to drag yourself to a job that leaves you feeling flat.

PART III

THE TOOLKIT:
THE 14 TOOLS FOR SUCCESS

CHAPTER 10

THE KEYS TO SUCCESS

"You can't put a limit on anything. The more you dream, the farther you get."

Michael Phelps
Olympic gold-medal swimmer

My research and consulting work show that the following key factors play a crucial part in manifesting success. Here they are:

1. WORK WITH A SUCCESS BUDDY OR SUCCESS SUPPORT GROUP

Foundational concept: We do not achieve success alone.

Isaac Newton (1676) said it well: "If I have seen further, it is by standing on the shoulders of giants."

When we study those who have succeeded, even people who appear to be loners or so-called "self-made men," we find they had help. Support is especially important when you embark on overcoming FOS. It is a formidable opponent that thrives on fear and negativity. To do battle with FOS, you need support. For that reason, I repeat my signature slogan:

> *Your Mind is a Dangerous Neighborhood,*
> *Don't Walk Around Alone.*
> *Get a Success Buddy!*

Make your journey easier. Commit to connecting, communicating and collaborating with a Success Buddy, Success Group and a Spiritual Partner. With proper support, you will defeat FOS and gain back your *joie de vivre.*

2. Nurture Your Spiritual Side

Foundational concept: We can reap benefits from nurturing our spiritual side.

To nurture your spiritual side, direct your focus inward to a path that reflects and embraces your deepest values about self, love, family, community and the larger world. Spirituality can be a source of inspiration and expansion of your inner life.

Nurturing your inner life may include practicing meditation, relaxation, breathing techniques, visualization, tuning into your intuition and learning how to use it, speaking your truth, and engaging in prayer and contemplation. These spiritual practices can help you connect to larger realities like nature, the divine realm, the self, and the whole human community.

Work with a Spiritual Partner who can help you examine your spirituality, genuine nature and core values. Nurturing your spiritual side gives you an opportunity to explore concepts such as virtue, love, honesty, respect, acceptance, patience, tolerance, compassionate regard for self and others, honor, harmony and forgiveness. In the process of self-discovery, the question of whether you believe in a deity comes to the surface, and the answer helps to sculpt your philosophy of living.

Over the centuries, the word "spiritual" was synonymous with "religious" or "religion." Today, the term spirituality is less focused on organized religions and more associated with exploring your inner life, your pure potential and the values you live by. Nurturing your spiritual side leads to inner knowledge and an ability to use one's intuition.

The spiritual journey is a quest to find the power of self. Deepak Chopra (2010) says that when you get in touch with your spiritual side "there is an absence of fear, no compulsion to control and no struggle for approval or external power."

3. CREATE AN INNER CIRCLE OF SUPPORT

Circle of Support

TOXIC CIRCLE
Untrustworthy people
Undermining, competitive, envious, resentful
Want to replace, one up or devalue you

AMBIVALENT CIRCLE
Skeptical people with doubts
Sometimes supportive with periodic misgivings
Have mixed feelings about your talent, vision & mission

OUTER CIRCLE
Inconsistently supportive people
Mostly supportive and encouraging
Can be negative, critical & judgmental

INNER CIRCLE
Trustworthy Partners, Family, Friends & Acquaintances
Consistently supportive and encouraging
Believe in your talent & vision

Foundational concept: We need a trustworthy Inner Circle of support and guidance to accompany us on the path to success.

Trustworthy partners, family, friends, acquaintances and colleagues who are supportive and encouraging help us to strive for and maintain success.

No matter where you are on the Success Continuum, you will benefit from an Inner Circle of support. I suggest you build a support system of five to ten people who have your back. Include your Success Buddy, Spiritual Partner and Success Support Group in your Inner Circle.

Surround yourself with people who will help you stay right sized in moments of triumph and steadfast when you need to overcome failures, obstacles and periods of self-doubt.

The Circle of Support diagram can help you think about the level of support you are or are not getting from the people around you. Keep the people in your Inner Circle close to you and move everyone else a distance away depending on their level of support and ability to show up for you. People who are toxic should not be in your life and should not have the ability to interact with you unless it is absolutely necessary, and you have no other choice.

(Read more about the Inner Circle and Circle of Support in Chapter 12: Tool 2: Create A Circle of Support.)

4. Practice Being Your Own Cheerleader

Foundational concept: We need to give ourselves positive feedback and learn how to become our own cheerleader.

Wherever you go, there you are. We cannot escape our own company. We cannot escape our own minds. We are inside ourselves 24/7, so we must learn how to soothe ourselves, convert fear into faith and incorporate the positive feedback of others and make it our own.

Practice giving yourself positive feedback and use the toolkit section to learn how to become your own cheerleader. Inherent in self-esteem is the ability to be supportive and encouraging to yourself. This skill is especially important when your Success Buddy, Spiritual Partner and Inner Circle people are not available. The moments you are on your own give you the opportunity to think positively, have faith in the process and believe in yourself fully.

5. PRACTICE THE *5As*

Foundational concept: To solve a problem, you have to recognize and accept that the problem exists.

Overcoming FOS depends on becoming conscious that you are in your own way and accepting when and how you engage in behaviors that are not in service of your goals.

The "5As", Awareness, Acceptance, Action, Accountability and Actualization, provide a step-by-step approach to overcoming FOS and moving into high performance. Practicing the 5As heightens your awareness about how FOS is operating in your work life and helps you observe and accept that you are sometimes behaving self-destructively. The 5As encourage you to create a realistic Action Plan, hold you accountable for that plan, and foster and facilitate self-actualization.

6. DO WHAT YOU LOVE

Foundational concept: Doing what you love is the natural outgrowth of tuning into your passion, turning passion into creative action and creating a Vision.

Tuning into your passion is the starting point if you want to use your natural gifts and live in your potential. Once you tune into your passion, you can move organically to doing what you love and following your bliss.

It's important to find ways to accelerate the process of tuning into your passion. While you can perform work that pays the bills, it's not the same as doing work you love.

If you already know your passion, focus on turning your passion into creative action. If you are unable to earn a prosperous living doing what you love, read the chapters on underearning or underachieving. (Chapter 5: Underearning; Chapter 6: Underachieving) Use the toolkit to overcome the FOS behaviors that prevent you from resolving these issues.

7. THINK PROSPEROUSLY

Foundational concept: Earning your living doing what you love requires prosperity thinking.

Prosperity thinking is faith-based thinking that involves optimism, hope, Vision, and affirmative thoughts about the self. It rests on the beliefs that "I can manifest the life I want," "There is more where that came from," and "There is enough for everyone."

Deprivation thinking (also known as scarcity thinking) is fear-based thinking that involves pessimism, negative futurizing (i.e., imagining negative outcomes or catastrophes), playing small (diminishing or devaluing your vision), and self-doubt. It rests on the beliefs that "There is not enough for everyone," and "There's a limited supply—so if *you* get something, it takes something away from *me*."

While prosperity thinking is based on the Law of Abundance and the idea that there is enough of everything for everyone, deprivation thinking is based on the Law of Scarcity and the idea that there are limited resources and only the few can benefit.

Deprivation thinking envisions small outcomes and contraction. Prosperous thinking envisions meaningful outcomes and expansion. The Inside Job suggests that you can manifest doing work you love that has meaning and purpose and is also economically rewarding. This doesn't mean you have to have millions of dollars. It means you earn well and are financially comfortable. This gives you an opportunity to thrive in your work life and live a prosperous life financially, emotionally, spiritually, and physically.

8. SUBLIMATE YOUR AGGRESSION

Foundational concept: High performance and long-term success depend on sublimated aggression.

Sublimated aggression is aggressive energy converted into positive, assertive, goal-oriented action. Think *Olympic Performance!*

Stay with me for a minute because I am reframing *aggression.* I am asking you to think of aggression as energy and sublimated aggression as energy converted into constructive action.

As a word and concept, aggression has a bad rap. It is commonly associated with anger, antagonism, assault, hostility, offensive speech or behavior, and violence.

Sublimated aggression is a term from the field of psychology. To sublimate means to "channel, redirect, or convert." *Sublimated aggression* is aggression converted into constructive action.

Sublimated aggression is positive. When we sublimate our aggressive drive (energy), we channel, convert or redirect our aggressive energy into: ambition, assertiveness, bravery, collaboration, communication, courage, creativity, determination, faith, focused action, fortitude, ingenuity, persistence, risk-taking, tenacity to face and overcome obstacles, and the willingness to be our authentic and genuine self.

Undisciplined aggression becomes acted-out anger, belligerence, contempt, control, desire to hurt or kill, disdain, impatience, intolerance, intimidation, oppositional and passive-aggressive behavior, prejudice, rebellion, resentment, withholding, withdrawal, violence and war.

To be successful on a reliable and consistent basis sublimate your aggression—convert it into constructive goal-oriented actions. When you do, you will find it your best friend and ally.

9. LIVE IN FAITH AND HOPE

Foundational concept: Success thrives on faith and hope and withers in the face of fear and despair.

Living in faith and visualizing positive outcomes will help you perform at your personal best and live in your potential. It is also an insurance policy against the two-headed monster: Fear and Despair. These toxic feeling states mute passion, devalue Vision, and paralyze action.

To counteract the toxic impact of fear and despair, you must turn fear into faith and despair into hope as quickly as possible. Franklin Delano Roosevelt (1933) said, "The only thing we have to fear is fear itself."

If you have ever done battle with fear, you know he was right. When we face fear head-on, we find that most of our fears are false or highly exaggerated.

If we release fear, F E A R becomes an acronym for **F**alse **E**vidence **A**ppearing **R**eal. So, face fear head-on, dismantle its falsehoods and use a positive acronym for F E A R: **F**orgetting **E**verything's **A**ll **R**ight.

10. Create A Solid Work Ethic

Foundational concept: Success depends on a solid work ethic based on taking reliable and consistent action.

Commit to your Vision, stay keenly focused on your goals, adopt a persistent attitude and live by the slogans, "If you don't try, you can't succeed," and "Never, never, never, never give up!"

High performers are committed to their goals and remain ambitious, creative, focused and determined to reach and stay at the top. You can get there, too!

Summary

These overarching keys to success work together to form the Inside Job approach. Incorporate the foundational concepts into your success toolkit and practice the underlying principles. You'll be glad you did!

Let's move on to the Toolkit.

CHAPTER 11

TOOL 1:
WORK WITH A
SUCCESS BUDDY

Your Mind is a Dangerous Neighborhood,
Don't Walk Around Alone.
Get a Success Buddy!

Judith F. Chusid
Signature Slogan

WHAT IS A SUCCESS BUDDY?

A Success Buddy is your personal cheerleader, action partner and advocate. The Success Buddy relationship is a reciprocal one. You are your Success Buddy's personal cheerleader, action partner and advocate.

Choose a Success Buddy using your sixth sense and your heart. Choose someone you intuitively feel is trustworthy and with whom you can be open, vulnerable and authentic.

The goal of the Success Buddy relationship is to foster positive action. Over time, your Success Buddy will come to understand what triggers your

FOS Signals and what feelings, thoughts or circumstances set off fear reactions.

Your Success Buddy will come to understand where on the Success Continuum you get stuck and will help you stay on track. Your job is to do the same for your buddy.

The Importance of Working with a Success Buddy

Success thrives on support, encouragement and feedback from a person who is "in our corner." Working with a Success Buddy is always important. When working on overcoming a career block like FOS, it is crucial.

FOS is a formidable opponent. It is the enemy of Vision, progress and self-actualization.

To stop playing small and live in your potential, you must put distance between yourself and FOS. A Success Buddy and Success Support Group are crucial helpers in this endeavor.

No one succeeds alone; success requires allies. You and your Success Buddy are allies and confidants. It is difficult, if not impossible, to overcome FOS without support. As they say these days, "It takes a Village!" Take your Success Buddy, Support Group and, if you so desire, a professional performance coach along with you. You'll be happy you did. I promise!

A Success Group

A Success Group provides support in a group setting. The group has advantages. It provides feedback from multiple people who have different personalities and points of view. More than one person understands how you get in your own way, and more people share your triumphs and struggles.

A PERSONAL STORY

One of my most influential Success Buddies, someone I lovingly call my Enthusiasm Buddy, pushed me to write this book. At the time of our meeting, I had already logged over thirty years of experience resolving resistances to success and fear of success issues as an educational consultant and university instructor, sports psychologist and performance enhancement coach working across industry lines. I also had been giving one-, three- and five-day workshops on a regular basis for years.

We met while I was researching how widespread FOS was among family, friends, colleagues, and friends of friends. I started a support group on the subject and began facilitating self-growth groups with a strict focus on resolving FOS.

She joined one of the groups and quickly became a fan of my work. She believed that FOS was a common problem and that the Inside Job approach had a built-in larger audience than I realized.

Like a broken record, she repeatedly said, "You have to write a book about FOS." She finally coined this phrase, "You are the Suze Orman of Fear of Success," and said it to me repeatedly. Frustrated with my lack of response and enthusiasm, she said, "I'm coming to your office to work on the first chapter. Be ready!"

I wrote some pages to placate her, but it was a meager effort. When she arrived, she began editing. As she deleted and added sentences, I experienced a volcanic feeling of outrage: *What does she know about FOS? I've been doing this for over thirty years! I'll write it!*

Of course, I wasn't actually angry at her. But in that moment, a competitive spirit arose in me and I claimed my work. Although I had to battle with my own FOS issues to put this book in your hands, I believe the years it has taken to write and rewrite this manuscript have led to a richer book.

My buddy's "Never, never, never give up" attitude was contagious, and I am grateful. Her enthusiasm and belief not only inspired this book, it led me to create the Success Is An Inside Job® company, grow the professional and self-growth workshops, and expand my work to larger audiences.

Even if you believe a Success Buddy or Group isn't right for you, I urge you to try it. I think you'll be very pleased you did.

How the Success Buddy System Works

Peer-to-peer help has a proven track record for problem solving and creativity. Humans have always banded together to do the tasks of living, surviving and fending off enemies.

We are built for collaboration. We band together for good causes and to overcome natural disasters, illnesses, grief, emotional issues, addictions, political crises, and business downturns. We barn-raise, build houses and celebrate together. We are good at inventing and creating in the service of progress and development. No high performer would prepare for competition without help.

Since we have such a rich tradition of supporting each other, why not help each other self-actualize? Your Success Buddy or Group can help you perform at your personal best and get to the top of your game.

The Success Buddy
or Success Support Group

You can choose to work with a Success Buddy *and* a Success Support Group. I highly recommend both.

For those who are more comfortable with a one-on-one relationship, a Success Buddy relationship is ideal. For those who are comfortable in groups and like the intellectual and emotional diversity of a group setting, a Success Group is perfect. Whether we choose to work with one person, a group or both, our buddies become essential to our success.

Working with an individual Success Buddy:

- Helps you deepen your understanding of FOS and how it interferes in your career or creative endeavors.
- Helps you track your FOS Signals.

- Helps you engage in behaviors that support your goals.
- Helps you create an Action Plan that is realistic.
- Helps you be accountable for your Action Plan in a firm but supportive manner.
- Helps you perform at your personal best.

Getting Support from a Success Group

Like the Success Buddy relationship, the goal of the Success Support Group is for members to help each other overcome FOS and self-sabotage. Group members help each other engage in behaviors that support their passion, Vision and mission. To accomplish this, group members must create a safe space for each member by giving honest and direct feedback that is supportive. Members agree to communicate with no criticism, negative judgment, sarcasm or impatience. The Group provides support and encouragement as each member acts as a compassionate witness to everyone's process.

A Group brings an added dimension to the buddy system. The benefits of working in a group setting are manifold.

You get all the benefits of working with an individual Success Buddy:

- Positive peer support.
- Encouragement to keep moving in the direction of your dreams and goals.
- Direct and honest feedback about your process.
- Clarity on how your FOS issues are interfering with your progress.

And you get additional perks:

- Multiple and diverse perspectives.
- Multiple personalities and experience.
- Experience communicating your needs and wants in a group setting.

- Practice observing yourself in a group setting—with curiosity rather than judgment.
- Practice in constructive communication and truth-telling skills and learning if and when you have issues.

Reciprocity

Whether you choose a Success Buddy, a Group or both, the relationship must be reciprocal. The buddy system is a two-way street. You must give as well as take from a Success Buddy or Group relationship. A reciprocal relationship depends on your being emotionally present and mentally invested in supporting your buddy or group members.

As I said earlier, I would not have written this book or launched my new company without my Enthusiasm Buddy and her unwavering belief that my work on FOS should become more visible. She, in turn, had my support to write, produce and perform a one-woman show. Reciprocally, the members of my two writers' groups would not have finished their works without peer-to-peer help.

Components of a Good Success Buddy Relationship

Your buddy or group provides a special kind of support. They will come to understand you in ways few people will. It is with your buddy or group that you can reveal your authentic self and showcase what you can produce. They are invested in helping you succeed, get to the top of your game, and live in your potential.

Good Success Buddies help each other stay on track. The same applies to Success Groups. Members help each other to keep moving in the direction of their goals. Buddy relationships gently push you to perform at your personal best.

You may be asking yourself, "Can I really achieve success?" and "Will a Success Buddy or Group help me get there?"

From personal experience, my answer is yes. From clinical and consulting experience, my answer is a resounding *YES*. Feedback from my students, clients and Success Is An Inside Job® Workshop participants is this: working with a Success Buddy, a Success Group or both makes everything easier, clearer and more possible. Your buddies appreciate your unique gifts and are inspired by your Vision.

Think of your Success Buddy or Success Group as your personal cheerleader. Your buddy or group become a caring witness to your process and your best advocate. Buddies and groups help you create an Action Plan and hold you accountable for implementing it. And accountability is very important because a Vision without action is a delusion.

The Secret to Success

As I said earlier, the big secret is this: *There is no secret to success.* Success is achieved through passion, Vision, determination, focus and hard work.

This quote from Picasso offers a golden truth: "The foundation of all success is action." The Buddy relationship can provide you with the essential support you need to take reliable and consistent actions in service of your goals.

We need others and they need us, to achieve our dreams, navigate rough waters and develop ways to overcome and outsmart our own resistances.

We benefit from the support of others. When we have it, we flourish!

Don't Play Small or Dumb Down Your Vision

Once you commit to stop playing small, overcome your fear of getting to the top of your game, and move in the direction of your goals, you have declared war on FOS, and it will fight back. It will try to outsmart you and use old tricks to interrupt momentum and oppose forward movement.

It's manipulative and sneaky. Much too powerful to combat alone. You must battle FOS with a "special ops" unit (to use a military term). Your Success Buddy, Support Group and Inner Circle comprise this unit. They will give you the emotional and mental support you need to move forward, take risks and stay in action.

Make Your Success Buddy or Success Group a Priority

The buddy system works if it becomes a priority. Commit to meeting with your Success Buddy or Success Group on a regular basis.

I suggest you set up a weekly format. Meet on the same day and time each week. Make the meeting sacred. Do not schedule anything in that time slot unless it's absolutely necessary and you have no other choice. If you're out of town on business or vacation, meet with your Success Buddy or Group by phone or internet.

Whether you experience success or stress, stay close to your support system. When making a big move forward, arrange for a daily check-in with your Success Buddy or Group. If you feel anxious or frightened, your support person or team can talk you off the ledge and help you stay focused.

Keep the following slogans in mind. When the going gets tough, a remembered slogan can help you save the situation:

- Life is a team sport—surround yourself with supportive people.
- Success Is An Inside Job®.
- Don't give up five minutes before the miracle.
- Don't give up five minutes after the miracle.
- Never, never, never, never give up.
- If you don't ask, you can't get.
- The foundation of all success is action.
- Action is the antidote to procrastination, fear and despair.
- "Try not. Do or do not. There is no 'try.' " (Lucas Films, 1980)
- Trying is dying—take action.

What If I Don't Believe in or Want a Success Buddy?

These tools are suggestions only. You can go your own way. If you are opposed to working with a Success Buddy or Group—don't do it.

However, if you want to challenge any cynical or pessimistic thoughts you have about this process, try taking a leap of faith. Ask someone to be an interim or temporary Success Buddy. Envision working with someone, whether you believe in it or not. Give it a chance and see if it helps. I think it will. Remember, you deserve the gift of an ally.

How Do I Find a Success Buddy or Group?

This relationship is important and should not be taken lightly. When you choose a Success Buddy, trust your intuition.

Look into your world. Make a list of people close to you: family and friends, colleagues, acquaintances from your spiritual or religious organization, community contacts, or parents of kids who know your kids. Move beyond your Inner Circle to others, like people in your neighborhood, or people you like and trust but haven't seen for a while. Peruse your list and select possible Success Buddy candidates. Then sort, screen and interview.

1. Schedule coffee dates with people you enjoy or have always wanted to get to know.
2. Mention you are working toward living in your career potential. Discuss your desire to "get out of your own way" and resolve any career or creative blocks you have. Give some common and non-threatening FOS examples that most people have, like procrastination or holding back in fear.
3. Mention this book and that the author recommends working with a Success Buddy. Listen carefully to the response.
4. Your potential buddy may react by:

a. Asking for more information (showing interest—a good sign).

b. Identifying with you and giving some personal information about FOS or a career block (indicating awareness he or she also has an issue—a good sign).

c. Making a joke or sarcastic remark (showing disdain—red flag).

d. Being defensive, saying something like "I don't have a fear of success" or "I'm lucky, I don't have any blocks." (demonstrating an armored attitude—red flag).

e. Making a critical remark about self-help books or the self-help movement (demonstrating a closed-minded and possibly arrogant attitude—red flag).

Clearly, only those responding in the "a" or "b" categories are potential Success Buddies.

Choosing a Success Buddy or Group

The choice of a Success Buddy is subjective and personal. It is very important to choose a person with whom you feel comfortable and safe. Your Success Buddy or Group should be excited about your Vision and have an attitude of acceptance and curiosity about your blocks. Your potential partner must be a "seeker" regarding his or her own life. By "seeker," I mean the person needs to have a desire for self-knowledge and improvement.

Good Success Buddies:

- Share openly and honestly.
- Take a pledge of confidentiality about what you share.
- Commit to meeting weekly on the same day and at the same time, in person, by phone or via the internet.
- Are accepting and nonjudgmental toward FOS issues.
- Give helpful and direct feedback in a kind, compassionate and courteous way.

- Are curious and interested to learn more about FOS and how it operates in their own lives.
- Want to help you resolve your FOS and have a strong desire to succeed and overcome their own self-sabotage.
- Are willing to ask for and accept your help and are honest if they can't help or don't know the answer.
- Have a sense of humor about their own issues and yours.
- Agree to be a true partner and read Success Is An Inside Job®, complete the recommended exercises, create an Action Plan, and work on identifying and overcoming FOS issues.

GROUND RULES FOR
SUCCESS BUDDIES AND GROUPS

TRUST

It is essential that you be able to share openly and honestly with your Success Buddy and members of your Success Group. You must establish trust so the relationship can flourish. Make a confidentiality pledge. Pledge out loud that whatever is said between you stays between you and your Success Buddy and/or Group unless you mutually agree otherwise.

COMMUNICATION AND FEEDBACK

Most of us communicate fairly well when we feel positive. But when we feel frustrated, conflicted, angry or disappointed, we have problems. So, you and your Buddy/Group need a constructive communication system for handling negative feelings. Remember to use words that are supportive, accepting and kind. Learn how to speak your truth and deliver difficult messages (such as how your Buddy is engaging in FOS Signals) in a manner that is not critical, judgmental, accusatory or blaming.

MEETING SCHEDULE & WORK FORMAT

Establish a weekly meeting schedule. In the beginning, it is best to start with a schedule of a couple of hours together, and then move to a weekly meeting of forty minutes to an hour.

For the first and second meetings, get to know each other. Share what your issues are and define your career or creative blocks. Discuss how FOS is showing up in your life. Try to identify and clarify your problem by naming how FOS is manifesting.

Are you underearning, underachieving, earning inconsistently, feeling pressured to overachieve, or upset by workaholism? At the higher levels of success, are you financially successful but unhappy, or having trouble reaching or maintaining a high level of performance? Are you in the beginning phase of derailing after you've reached the top?

During the introductory meetings, give each other information about your work history. Discuss your skills, talents, creativity and how you have and have not capitalized on them. Showcase your work life, "warts and all." Make sure in the first three meetings that you've read Chapters 1 through 3, completing the FOS Checklists and identifying your FOS Signals.

By the second or third week, you should be able to move toward a fifty-minute or one-hour format, each person taking half the talking time. Discuss what you're working on that week or month. It is ideal to meet in person, but if it isn't possible, make a phone or internet meeting on the same day and time each week.

USING THE WEEKLY FORMAT

1. Read this book together and bring any other sources of information into your weekly meeting (books, articles, videos, courses, retreats).
2. Take five minutes each, at the beginning of the meeting, to summarize the week. Be sure to identify any FOS Signals you engaged in.

3. Do the recommended exercises before you get to the meeting. Then both share your writing and what you've read. Questions to ponder before the meeting: Did I identify with the chapter or passage? What impact did the exercise have on me?

4. Before you end the meeting: 1) decide which chapter you'll read or reread; and 2) commit to the actions you will take that week.

Make it a priority to identify your FOS Signals. List each signal you use. Begin to track when and how often they appear. It is not unusual to have ten or more signals operating on a daily basis.

WORKING WITH SUCCESS BUDDIES REPRESENTS SELF-CARE

Success takes dedication, courage and passion. While work success is regarded as a good thing to achieve and can provide us with many rewards, success also heralds negative outcomes.

For instance, increased visibility can be very uncomfortable. You will likely feel increasingly vulnerable to scrutiny, criticism, jealousy, envy, anger and the competitive feelings of others.

Your Success Buddy or Success Group can cushion you from the negativity and help you stay centered and perform at your personal best while you navigate the landscape and pressures of success.

The buddy system, with its long-established history and track record of providing acceptance, emotional support, and confidentiality really works. It also provides you with a person who sees and values your gifts.

This unique and special relationship will bolster who you are (imperfections and all) and support your passion and Vision. Your Success Buddy and Group will encourage you to follow your bliss.

A supportive Success Buddy or Group will help you create a prosperous work life that is free from self-sabotage or serious self-destructive behaviors that can derail success.

Give the buddy system a try. What do you have to lose?

CHAPTER 12

TOOL 2: CREATE A CIRCLE OF SUPPORT

"No man is an island. No one is self-sufficient; everyone relies on others."

John Donne
17th Century Poet
From "Devotions Upon Emergent Occasions
and Seuerall Steps in my Sicknes"
—Meditation XVII, 1624

CIRCLE OF SUPPORT

A circle of support refers to the people who support and encourage you to be your authentic self, use your natural talents and gifts, find your purpose and live in your potential.

Why Create A Circle of Support?

Striving for success is an exciting journey of triumphs, victories and elation peppered with failure, disappointments and periods of no visible progress. To weather the highs and lows and ups and downs, it is important to surround yourself with trustworthy supporters who can help you stay right sized, centered and focused on your purpose.

We are all vulnerable at both ends of the Success Continuum; not just those of us who experience FOS. Times of triumph and high success put us in jeopardy of slipping into feelings of grandiosity, arrogance and entitlement (becoming demanding or acting as if we are above the rules). In times of failure or stagnation, we are in danger of falling into despair, self-doubt and depression.

In both circumstances, your Success Buddy and members of your support group and Inner Circle can help you stay centered, grateful and dedicated to your goals while still supporting you to be true to yourself.

"Thank You, But I Can Handle This on My Own!"

You argue, "Isn't it good to be self-reliant?" You ask, "Why do I need all this support?" My answer is this: It is difficult to stop FOS from broadcasting "fake news" and engendering fear and discouragement. Your best chance to combat FOS is with a Success Buddy or Group. Repeat my signature slogan: "Your mind is a dangerous neighborhood. Don't walk around alone. Get a Success Buddy."

To prove a point, let's see how well "going it alone" has worked for public figures, entrepreneurs, people in the business world, entertainers and performers who crash or slip into periods of low or dysfunctional performance. Not having the right support was self-destructive.

We are inundated with news about how individuals, companies and teams sabotage their success. It doesn't stop there, either. Everyday people, like you and me, are privy to the highs and lows of family, friends, peers and colleagues. We see people holding back in fear, acting self-destructively and not using their talents and skills.

The best way to protect yourself is to be proactive! Surround yourself with trustworthy and reliable supporters who are dedicated to helping you succeed. Let's see how.

Circle of Support (COS)

The COS diagram will help you think about your support system and assess the people around you. Use the diagram to distinguish those who are trustworthy and supportive *from* those who are not. You can also use it to assess how supportive you are to yourself.

In the Keys to Success section, you learned that support from a Success Buddy, Spiritual Partner and Inner Circle is a crucial to combating FOS and a key component of success. Trustworthy supporters endorse and encourage your work and act as loving witnesses to your process. They bolster and foster even in the face of setbacks and failures. I also talked about how important it is to be our own cheerleader.

The COS diagram is composed of four rings. The center, the bull's-eye, is the most important circle. It's the Inner Circle composed of trustworthy, reliable supporters. The three other rings, the Outer, Ambivalent and Toxic Circles, describe people whose support is inconsistent, skeptical or toxic.

Familiarize yourself with each circle. Read the definitions and then assess the people around you. Put each person in the category that describes how supportive or non-supportive they are to you. Then turn your attention to yourself and assess how supportive or unsupportive you are to yourself.

THE INNER CIRCLE

The Inner Circle is composed of people who are consistently supportive, unswerving in their belief in you and have your best interest in mind.

Members of your Inner Circle see your splendor and are invested in helping you live in your potential. Build an Inner Circle composed of your Success Buddy and Spiritual Partner and five to ten others (partners, family, friends and acqaintances) who will support and encourage you to keep moving forward and help you disengage from self-sabotage and *not* act out on FOS Signals.

Members of the Inner Circle are hardy. Nothing you say or do will discourage them from supporting you. They are trustworthy and dependable. They are people who are reliable. They believe in you and want you to use your gifts to the fullest and perform at your personal best. The people in your Inner Circle are encouraging, positive, and upbeat under all conditions. They do not become discouraged or negative when you experience brownout or blackout periods, i.e., when it appears it is futile to continue, or when the actions you take yield little or no results. Most importantly, your Inner Circle supports you when you feel despairing or experience a setback or failure. In fact, they see failure as an opportunity or a challenge to overcome.

Think of the members of your Inner Circle as personal cheerleaders and fans. When building your Inner Circle, put your Success Buddy and Spiritual Partner front and center. Next, add family, friends, colleagues, co-workers, and neighbors. You can even cultivate an acquaintance to become part of your Inner Circle. You do not have to know someone well or for many years to invite him/her into your Inner Circle. And, quality trumps quantity. Choose your Inner Circle carefully. Each person needs to believe in your talent, your soul's purpose, your Vision and your mission.

Many of you already have an Inner Circle or have the beginning of an Inner Circle. Talk to those close to you and ask if they will make a commitment to support you to live in your potential and help you resolve self-sabotage. Trust your intuition. You will know who belongs and who doesn't.

THE OUTER CIRCLE

The second ring is called the Outer Circle. This ring is composed of people who are generally supportive but periodically become negative, skeptical, critical or judgmental. I label these people as inconsistently supportive. While members of the Outer Circle are predominantly supportive, they lack consistency and predictability. They can cheerlead one minute and turn into a critic the next. On the positive side, you can gain a lot from their support. On the negative side, there is no way to predict when a member of the Outer Circle will bring you down or interfere with your momentum, mood, and enthusiasm. How you choose to utilize the support and interact with those in the Outer Circle depends on how conscious and realistic you are about what each person can give you. Proceed with caution and always take care of yourself.

THE AMBIVALENT CIRCLE

Move the ambivalent people a significant distance from you. They belong in the third ring. Not sure about who the ambivalent people are? Use the dictionary definition to clarify. Webster defines ambivalent as "having mixed feelings or contradictory ideas about something or someone." Synonyms for ambivalence are: uncertain, unsure, doubtful, indecisive, inconclusive, irresolute, of two minds, torn, undecided, in a quandary, on the fence, hesitating, wavering, vacillating, equivocating, blowing or running hot and cold.

Move all people who display ambivalent feelings or ideas toward you, your Vision, your talent or your goals into the Ambivalent Circle. Make sure you have minimal contact with them or contact only on an *as needed basis.*

THE TOXIC CIRCLE

We all know toxic people. The label speaks for itself. Toxic people are psychologically poisonous and have the potential to cause you great harm. Move those people far away from you. They are judgmental, competitive, angry, and jealous. Some have toxic envy, which is potentially very dangerous for you. If possible, do not have contact with any of these people, at all! If you must, have contact only when it's absolutely necessary.

When it comes to the Toxic Circle, institute strict guidelines, self-regulation and self-discipline. A rule of thumb is this: Do not give any information to people in the Toxic Circle. Do not give information to people who have contact with them.

People in the Toxic Circle are not your friend and do not have your best interest in mind. They either want to replace you, take you down or see you fall or fail. Your splendor makes them feel small, inadequate or competitive (in an unhealthy way). People in the Toxic Circle not only want what you have, they want to be who you are. Their goal is to eliminate you and take your place. Keep your distance.

ASSESS WHO IS AROUND YOU

Use the COS diagram and the definitions to assess who is around you. Your core support emanates from the Inner Circle comprised of your Success Buddy, Spiritual Partner, Success Support Group and five to ten people who believe in you. The people in your Inner Circle are consistently trustworthy and supportive. Move everyone else away from you depending on their level of support and ability to show up for you.

INNER CIRCLE CANDIDATES

Be on the lookout for Inner Circle candidates. The Inside Job approach recommends you build a solid team of people for the Inner Circle. Use the tips from the Success Buddy section to build your Inner Circle. At first blush, someone might seem an unlikely candidate for your Inner Circle. People can surprise us! Someone not on your Inner Circle list may demonstrate they are supportive. You never know. And you don't have to know them for a long time. It can happen with a new acquaintance, a colleague, or a neighbor. Keep your heart open and you will find people to fill your Inner Circle.

Circle of Support

TOXIC CIRCLE
Untrustworthy people
Undermining, competitive, envious, resentful
Want to replace, one up or devalue you

AMBIVALENT CIRCLE
Skeptical people with doubts
Sometimes supportive with periodic misgivings
Have mixed feelings about your talent, vision & mission

OUTER CIRCLE
Inconsistently supportive people
Mostly supportive and encouraging
Can be negative, critical & judgmental

INNER CIRCLE
Trustworthy Partners, Family, Friends & Acquaintances
Consistently supportive and encouraging
Believe in your talent & vision

Assessment

The COS diagram and circle descriptions will help you assess who is around you. In addition, assess how supportive or unsupportive you are to yourself. What are your inner voices like? Where are you on the trust continuum? Are you trustworthy and supportive of yourself? Or, are you inconsistent, ambivalent or toxic to yourself? Inner voices that sound like people in the Outer, Ambivalent or Toxic Circles, will sabotage your passion, Vision, self-esteem and talent.

Use the assessment exercise below to categorize the people around you. Share your assessment list with your Success Buddy, Spiritual Partner and Inner Circle.

EXERCISE: Use the COS Diagram to Assess Those Around You and Yourself

1. Make a list of people who have some influence in your work life or have any input into your career (partners, family friends, peers, colleagues, acquaintances, people in your neighborhood and congregation, and community members). Use the descriptions above and put everyone in your life into one of the four circles.
2. Think about who is closest to you and stretch to those who have the most casual relationship with you.
3. Assess yourself.

CHAPTER 13

TOOL 3: NURTURE YOUR SPIRIT & BODY

"mens sana in corpore sano"
(A healthy mind, in a healthy body)

Satires of Juvenal
(CE 0.345–64)

Good self-care depends on us taking care of our bodies and nourishing our spiritual nature. That means, we need to eat well, exercise, and look after our spiritual lives.

Tool 3 reminds us that the mind-body connection is powerful, and it is important to take care of ourselves physically and spiritually. Many of us have heard the slogan, "Take care of your body; if you don't, where will you live?" It reflects the wisdom that our mental, psychological and spiritual states are connected. How we feel and what we think affects our physical health.

Modern medicine has learned what ancient medicine has known for centuries, that certain physical illnesses and conditions are psychologically induced. They can develop as a result of stress. For example, ulcers, irritable bowel syndrome (IBS), and certain types of migraine headaches are stress related conditions. Stress and unhappiness drain us psychologically and deplete our spirit. To fortify your physical health and strengthen your immune system, nurture your spiritual side.

Spiritual practices such as meditation and physical practices such as yoga and tai chi can calm our minds and promote better physical health. It is impossible to have a flourishing career if you are physically ill or out of shape. So, take care of your body. Make sure you get enough sleep and exercise. Create healthy eating habits and keep stress to a minimum.

While it is impossible to eliminate all stress from our lives, we can create support systems and learn skills that help us handle stress better. Being proactive helps. A proactive approach gives you the opportunity to put a plan in place for handling difficult or challenging relationships, work conditions or life circumstances.

Nurturing Your Spiritual Side

We all have a spiritual life, whether we are conscious of it or not. When we use our natural talents, skills and abilities, we honor an important aspect of our spiritual essence.

Applying spiritual principles to our work life allows us to do what we love with integrity, heartfelt intentions and a value system we believe in and respect.

Integrating spiritual principles into our work life is advocated by spiritual teachers and advocates. They recommend practicing spiritual principles in all our affairs, which includes work.

Emily Bennington, (2017) a teacher of contemplative practices, recommends integrating spiritual principles into our everyday work life in her book, *Miracles at Work: Turning Inner Guidance into Outer Influence.* Marianne Williamson live-streamed a three-day workshop called *Creating a Career That Matters: The Inner Keys to Outer Success,* discussing resolving career blocks from a spiritual perspective.

I believe doing work you love and following your bliss is a spiritually inspired experience. Following your bliss requires holding on to your beliefs and moving confidently in the direction of your dreams. This requires action, as Henry David Thoreau (1854) said:

> "If you have built castles in the air, your work need not be lost; that is where they should be. Now put the foundations under them."

What is the foundation dreams rest upon? The foundation under dreams is prosperity thinking, also referred to as abundance thinking. This spiritual concept is based on faith, hope and optimism. In fact, the word "prosperity" comes from the Latin, *pro* (for) and *spero* (hope), which translates literally to "for hope" or "toward hope."

Prosperity and abundance are spiritual ways of thinking and being. The goal is not to acquire money or wealth, although we can. The goal is to become a prosperous person defined as one who is fully functioning and lives in his or her potential.

Building spiritual muscles helps us practice prosperity thinking in our lives so we can live in a spiritual flow and envision a positive future. We can all benefit from living in prosperity thinking.

When we do work we love, we give ourselves a daily opportunity to use our talents in a meaningful way and to apply spiritual principles to our work life. When we merge meaningful work with spiritual principles, we are practicing "spiritual economics."

Spiritual economics is the economic exchange that occurs when you share your talents with the world with integrity and consideration of others. The exchange is simple: you offer your skills to the world and get paid. In turn, you pay others for their contributions whether that comes in the form of a service or product. That is the natural ebb and flow of the economic exchange.

SPIRITUAL ECONOMICS

Spiritual economics is a way of thinking and being where we apply spiritual principles to our work life. In the broader view, it can apply to our economic system. Movements like Conscious Capitalism and Impact Investing have already folded spiritual principles into their philosophies. While this may seem overly idealistic for our capitalistic, free enterprise system, I prefer to believe it is doable both on an individual basis and on a larger scale.

Early proponents of Spiritual Economics were Charles Filmore, (2012) author of *Prosperity: Spiritual Secrets to an Abundant Life*, and Eric Butterworth, (2001) who wrote *Spiritual Economics*.

These spiritual teachers encourage us to nurture our spiritual side and bring spirituality into everything we do, including our work life, to produce prosperity and abundance. I believe practicing spiritual economics is essential to thriving. We need this individually, as a society and as stewards of our planet.

While I am not an economist, I believe if we infuse free enterprise with Spiritual Economics, we would be practicing *Spiritual Capitalism*. (Rensler, 2006; Hendren, 2007) I define Spiritual Capitalism as doing business for profit (or not-for-profit) without engaging in greed or exploitation. While this may seem like a utopian idea, I think it is an idea we can all work to bring about.

Spiritual Capitalism and Spiritual Economics, is a way of reimagining how we can do business. The law of prosperity is at the core of these principles. Incorporating spiritual principles into our work means we do business with integrity. It means we deliver a good service or product and put our most important resource, people, first. We put their economic health and welfare above all else.

I do not want to imply that I think making money is bad or dirty. This is far from the truth. I am suggesting that we do *the business of making money* according to spiritual principles rather than narcissistic/selfish/greedy principles.

In my reimagining, Spiritual Economics rests on three important concepts: 1) do work you love; 2) think of work as performing a service for others; 3) do business without exploiting colleagues, co-workers, consumers, employees or yourself.

Doing business according to spiritual principles rests on prosperity thinking which is based on the concept that there is enough for everyone and there is more where that came from. Spiritual economics posits we can all earn a comfortable living sharing our talents, skills and abilities with each other. It's what we are here to do.

Build Spiritual Muscles—
Work with a Spiritual Partner

Building your spiritual muscles creates infinite possibilities. When you nurture your spirituality, it is easier to face and overcome failures, obstacles and the tendency to self-sabotage. You feel more centered and authentic. You boost and strengthen your self-esteem and self-worth. Just as your psyche is a container for your personality and emotions, your spiritual side is a container for your values and your highest self. It's an integral part of sharing your gifts with others.

At the Success Is An Inside Job® Workshops, each participant is assigned a Spiritual Partner, as well as a Success Buddy. Spiritual Partners meet daily throughout the week to discuss spiritual principles and how they can be integrated into work. Participants love this part of the workshop and they say it brings an added dimension to their work. Interestingly, spiritual principles are already at work when people arrive. It never seems to matter at all that Spiritual Partners are arbitrarily assigned to one another. The partnerships work.

To explore the area of spirituality, try the following:

1. Take a leap of faith and jump into the arena of spirituality, even if you are ambivalent or do not relate to the idea.
2. Invite someone to be your Spiritual Partner. Use the same tips

and techniques you employed to find a Success Buddy, and remember:

a. Choose someone with whom you feel comfortable and trust.

b. Choose someone who is interested in exploring spirituality and someone who is interested in nurturing his or her spiritual side.

c. Choose someone nonjudgmental who will support you in your journey to self-actualize.

Explore Spirituality with Your Spiritual Partner

Explore spiritual principles by sharing your spiritual practice and philosophy with your Spiritual Partner. If you don't have a spiritual practice or philosophy, explore the concept of spirituality and discuss how you can learn more about the topic.

Here's an exercise to get you started. Share with your Spiritual Partner in your weekly meeting.

EXERCISE: What Does Spirituality Mean to Me?

1. What is my understanding of spirituality?
2. Do I have a spiritual life? (If yes, describe it. If no, tell your thoughts on why not.)
3. Identify and describe your spiritual source.
4. What is the source of your internal inspiration?

Next think about questions like, "Do I believe in a power greater than myself?" and "When I need strength, comfort and hope to aspire to being my highest self, where do I turn?" This exercise helps to deepen your understanding of spirituality and, if you want to, sculpt a concept of higher power.

EXERCISE: Spirituality, You, and Work

Answer the questions below and share with your Spiritual Partner. These questions can provide you with a forum for deepening your spiritual side, thinking about where your hope and inspiration comes from, and creating a brand of spirituality you can take into your work life.

1. How can nurturing your spiritual side help you in your work or creative life?
2. Do you believe in a power greater than yourself such as G-d, a specific spiritual philosophy (Buddhism, Native American Principles, Christianity, Judaism, the Kabbala), or some force in the Universe that provides a "helping hand"?
3. Do you call on a power greater than yourself to help you manifest your Vision and reach your goals? (If yes, describe it. If no, tell your thoughts on why not.)
4. What spiritual practice would you like to put into your daily routine? (Think about meditation, yoga, reading or listening to podcasts about spirituality, prosperity and living in one's potential.)

Ways to Boost Your Spirituality and Physical Health

1. Develop a practice of daily meditation.
2. Add some form of moving meditation/exercise to your weekly routine: yoga, tai chi, bicycling, swimming, running moderately, or walking.
3. Enrich your spiritual life: take a prosperity course, join a group that discusses and fosters spirituality, read books and listen to podcasts that focus on the mind-body connection and spirituality.
4. Create a healthy food plan that contains fresh fruit, vegetables, protein and grains. Stay away from processed food and sugar.

5. Exercise at least three times a week at home or in a gym.
6. Go for medical and dental check-ups on a regular basis.
7. Add holistic practitioners and practices to your wellness routine: acupuncture, Chinese medicine, regular massages, etc.

Stay in a healthy state of mind and spirit and you will find it is easier to move in the direction of your dreams and follow your bliss. When your body is in top physical condition, you feel energized. When your spiritual side feels centered and at one with the Universe, you have the psychic energy and creativity to live in your potential and perform at your personal best.

Tool 4: Practice the 5As: Awareness, Acceptance, Action, Accountability, Actualization

"Better to do something imperfectly than to do nothing flawlessly."

Robert H. Schuller

The first step to solving a problem is to become conscious you have one. The solution depends on recognizing how the problem operates and creating a step-by-step Action Plan to overcome it. The Inside Job 5As provide a progressive way to do this. They are:

- Awareness
- Acceptance
- Action
- Accountability
- Actualization

You have already begun the process of Awareness and Acceptance. In the previous chapters, we defined FOS and described how it operates. You had an opportunity to decide if FOS is your issue. The FOS checklists and achievement graphs provided additional data to help you decide if FOS is operating in your work life. As you continued to read, you deepened your understanding of the various symptoms of FOS.

At this point in your journey of self-discovery, I think you realize that your work issue is not the result of bad luck, a shaky economy, a dysfunctional family, or growing up on the wrong side of the tracks. FOS is *your* problem and you are stuck in unhealthy patterns of self-sabotage because it is actively operating in your life. As Pogo said, "We have met the enemy, and he is us." (Kelly, 1975)

Getting out of your own way and living up to your potential can put you off balance and should not be done alone. Enlisting the help of a Success Buddy or Success Group, will help you move forward more comfortably.

While moving forward is exciting and filled with potential, it can also feel scary and ego-deflating. Moving forward requires a significant amount of initiative and energy you may not be used to expending. This is difficult, if not impossible, to do alone. Discovering you have unconsciously been the architect of your own self-defeating patterns can be hard to face.

Facing the truth can be unnerving and intimidating. Have no fear! We have all been through it and with your Success Buddy at your side, you will have the support you need to overcome fear, regret or self-criticism. With the support of your Success Buddy, you can confront aspects of your personality you would rather deny, minimize or avoid. While this process might appear like a tall order, it is manageable *because* you do it together.

When you engage in this process, you will discover you have the power to change your work life. The Awareness and Acceptance steps of the 5As allow you to become conscious. In your new state of awareness, you can make a revolutionary discovery: There are no victims, only volunteers.

You can defeat FOS by reaching higher levels of awareness. FOS can only operate effectively in the dark, in the unconscious. FOS thrives when it operates unconsciously. Once we shine a light on it, it loses power. The 5As help make your unconscious conscious.

Tool 4: Practice the 5As

The 5As help clarify the reality of FOS. You cannot tackle a problem unless you know it's there.

Remember: FOS operates unconsciously. While you have a conscious desire to succeed, your unconscious experiences fear and ambivalence and makes a plan to interrupt your momentum or move you away from success.

I can assure you of this: If you are sabotaging yourself anywhere on the Success Continuum *or* after reaching the heights of your profession, you are suffering from FOS and are most likely not conscious of the emotional impact, pressures and fears that come with the territory of achieving success.

Who's Responsible—Me?

At this point, you may ask, "Am I responsible for being stuck?" The answer: "Yes, you are!" This is good news and bad news. Bad news first: it means you have been the architect of your own pain. You and you alone engaged in self-defeating patterns. You were in your own way. You were unable to honor your gifts and be in your own power. You were uncomfortable with some aspect of success and engaged in some form of self-sabotage.

The good news is that FOS does not have to run the show anymore. When you do the Inside Job, you move forward. Working with a Success Buddy, doing the exercises and developing new behaviors, puts you on a new track. You stop surviving and start thriving. Releasing yourself from "victimhood" is a powerful, life-changing step.

To do this you need a good plan. This is the third step in the 5As: Action. Action is everything. It's the foundation of success. Without action, nothing gets accomplished. Sitting around dreaming will not help you accomplish your goals. A dream without action is a delusion. Create a solid action plan and remind yourself that action is the key to progress.

A Developmental Look at Action

We are born to take action. As babies, our first "action" is crying. We cry to alert our caretakers that we need attention. Jean Piaget (1923) writes that the first steps in self assertion and cognitive development happen when babies "act on the environment." That means babies begin to take action early in their development. They reach for things. They swat at the mobile hanging over their cribs. They try to raise their heads even when their muscles can't fully support them. They crawl as soon as they're able to "get somewhere."

We humans are built to move forward and act on the environment. We have a natural desire to "do something" and "get somewhere." Every parent knows that as soon as kids can walk or run, they walk or run away from us, not toward us. They are moving into a bigger, more expanded life.

When we look at people who are successful, we see that they take constructive action on a reliable and consistent basis. The Action step will help you do the same. Action is like air; you need it to breathe life into your potential. Again, here is where your Success Buddy is invaluable. Together, you'll create an Action Plan: a set of actions that move you incrementally to your goal.

Action has another aspect. It is the antidote to procrastination, depression, despair, and the status quo. Whenever you feel stuck, take an action. Any constructive action will catapult you out of the doldrums and into a more optimistic mood.

However, creating an Action Plan is not enough. You need to execute and hold yourself accountable. A solid work ethic is one of the ten keys to success, and it's a significant one. It brings us to the Accountability step of the 5As. This step is where your Success Buddy helps you stay on track, while remaining your ally and cheerleader.

In the Accountability stage, you and your Success Buddy help each other stay focused. It's extremely important to continue your weekly meetings because you are familiar with the FOS Signals each of you employs. As your work together progresses, you become more and more knowledgeable about each other's FOS "tricks" and are able to anticipate when self-defeating patterns might be activated.

The 5As Summarized

Practicing Awareness, Acceptance, Action and Accountability brings about self-realization and self-Actualization. You begin to live more and more in your potential.

AWARENESS: NAME IT

In **Awareness**, you identify your FOS behaviors and any other issue that may be contributing to your work problem or dilemma. In the Awareness stage, you come face to face with your issues, letting go of denial, minimization and rationalization. You are naming your problem with clarity and accuracy.

ACCEPTANCE: CLAIM IT

In **Acceptance**, you own the problem—you "claim it" to be your own. In the Acceptance stage, you start to see your FOS more clearly, moving it from your unconscious mind to your conscious mind. You transition to a high state of ownership and visibility about your problem. You look FOS squarely in the eye and say, "I see how you operate." You accept the truth and look at the behaviors that create problems.

ACTION & ACCOUNTABILITY: WORK IT

The **Action** and **Accountability** steps are all about taking actions that defeat FOS and support living in your potential. This is the "work it" stage.

When you actively use the Action and Accountability steps, you deactivate FOS and render it powerless to interfere with your life.

Following the 5A system builds hope, faith and confidence. This is important, because FOS chips away at all three and thrives in the dark. The first four steps of the 5As shine a light on darkness and illuminate the unconscious. Like all resistances, FOS cannot flourish in the light. It only has power when it operates below your conscious radar.

Practicing Awareness, Acceptance, Action and Accountability makes the unconscious conscious. When you become aware of the feelings and thoughts you repressed or suppressed, you give yourself the opportunity to feel the fear and ambivalence you have about achieving success. You also give yourself the opportunity to observe your FOS Signals in action and understand their power to sabotage you.

Practicing Awareness, Acceptance, Action and Accountability is an optimistic endeavor that yields these benefits:

- You stop acting out on your FOS Signals.
- You lower your fear and ambivalence about success.
- You begin to live in your potential.

SELF-ACTUALIZATION

The Self-Actualization Formula
Awareness + Acceptance + Action + Accountability = Self-Actualization

If your goal is to self-actualize, working the first 4As will lead you there.

- Heighten your awareness by working with your Success Buddy and Spiritual Partner.
- Raise your acceptance level by clarifying and owning your behavior.
- Create an Action Plan that is realistic, manageable and matched to your goals.
- Be accountable to your Success Buddy (or any other support person or group) for enacting your Action Plan.

It will work, if you work for it. Put one foot in front of the other and keep moving forward; eventually the light bulb of awareness will go on. You will have "Aha" moments and come face to face with your personal power—your ability to use your natural talents to create your right liveli-hood and follow your bliss. This only happens when you make a conscious decision to practice the 5As. This commitment is a pledge to perform at your personal best and do the work you feel destined to do in this life.

Heightening your Awareness

To heighten your **Awareness** about how FOS is operating in your life, try these techniques:

1. Review your FOS Signals Checklist.
    a. Discuss each of your signals with your Success Buddy.
    b. Focus on the FOS Signals that are active, and the circumstances and times you're most likely to engage in these behaviors.
    c. Group the FOS Signals by category (self-esteem issues, fears, etc.).
    d. Review your achievement-charting exercises.
        i. Discuss school achievement and any habits, behaviors, attitudes, or beliefs that were helpful or hindering in the past that still continue today.
        ii. Discuss your career achievement chart and any habits, behaviors, attitudes, or beliefs that were helpful or hindering in the past that still operate today.
2. Become aware of your tendency to argue, dispute or reject the truth. Your Success Buddy can help you identify:
    a. Denial (refusing to accept reality).
    b. Minimizing ("it's not that bad").
    c. Rationalizing (making excuses or coming up with a very good "case" for what you're doing).

The purpose of Awareness is to shed light on self-defeating and self-sabotaging behaviors such as remaining confused about your dream or Vision, giving up on your Vision, or staying in a job or career that is emotionally draining and spiritually depleting.

Taking Ownership

The Acceptance stage is about ownership. In this stage, you are out of denial and confusion. You stake your claim to the problem. You accept responsibility for your behavior. You accept how FOS works and under what circumstances it operates. In the Acceptance stage, it is very important to be gentle with yourself. Continue to:

- Face yourself honestly and with compassion.
- Think with an open mind without being judgmental or critical of yourself.
- Substitute faith for fear.

Self-discovery flourishes in an atmosphere of love, acceptance and humor. Be good to yourself! Do not criticize, reprimand or reproach yourself for past actions. Don't *should* on yourself with, "I should have done this . . ." or "I should have done that."

When you refrain from beating yourself up for what you could have or should have done, you can make use of hindsight, which is very wise. Learning from the past is a key component to moving forward. Hindsight will help you heal, as well as level your FOS Signals.

You may not have used your gifts consistently. You may have acted self-destructively. Who hasn't? If you could have done something differently, you would have. Criticizing yourself won't help you build confidence, esteem or a feeling of inherent self-worth. So, try some loving acceptance.

Affirm this: *I am a unique and creative person with something special to contribute to the world.*

It's time to declutter your internal life and make room for a more empowered, more visible, more confident you. Discard behaviors, beliefs and attitudes that don't serve you anymore. Move unsupportive people away from you. If they are in your Inner Circle, gently move them to the outer rings. Detach with love from their negativity.

Awareness and Acceptance will deepen your journey of self-discovery. Study your history. While the past informs the present, it need not predict the future. You can *change your stars*[5] and build a new life.

Try examining FOS from this vantage point: Do a fear inventory. This will give you the opportunity to study how you think, what you feel and what you tend to do when in a state of fear. Fear typically forces us into taking defensive actions that are not in our best interest. It's enormously helpful to discover how you react when you're afraid.

Getting into Action

When you move into the action stage, it best to clarify your short and long-term goals and create an Action Plan. An Action Plan is a specific set of actions that move you incrementally toward your goal. A step-by-step plan helps you take the next right action and make consistent progress. Begin now by using the Career Action Plan template on the following page.

ACCOUNTABILITY

In the Accountability stage, you report the actions you are taking to your Success Buddy or Success Group. In this stage, it is important to declare what you're going to do   and do it!

Follow the sage advice Yoda gave Luke Skywalker in *The Empire Strikes Back*: "Do or do not! There is no try."

---

5 "Changing your stars" is a medieval term and another way of saying "you can change your destiny." In medieval England, it was very difficult to change economic or class status. It was believed at the time (and many still believe) that your destiny (or stars, as in astrology) is mapped out before you are born.

Career Action Plan

Today's Date: _____

THE ACTION PLAN

An action plan is a set of actions that are meant to move you incrementally toward your goal. It is important to create an action plan that is realistic and doable. Work with your Success Buddy or someone from your Inner Circle to develop actions that will help you advance forward.

GOALS

In the space below, list three short-term and three long-term goals.

Short-Term Goals	Long-Term Goals
1.	1.
2.	2.
3.	3.

30-DAY ACTION LIST

List six (6) actions that will support you in moving toward your goal in the next month.

Action:	Complete by:
1.	1.
2.	2.
3.	3.
4.	4.
5.	5.
6.	6.

Weekly Meeting Plan with Success Buddy
Day: _____   Time: _____
How _____(In-Person or By Phone or Internet)

BOOKEND YOUR ACTIONS

Bookending is a tool that helps you take action. To bookend, you call, email or text your Success Buddy or action partner before you take action to say that you are starting the action. You repeat this when you've completed the action or set of actions. Bookending is useful if you tend to procrastinate, or feel too discouraged, overwhelmed or frightened to take action.

ACCOUNTABILITY STEPS

1. Create a reasonable Action Plan with your Success Buddy or Group.
2. Bookend your actions.
3. Meet with your Success Buddy or Group weekly.
4. Lean on your Inner Circle, your Success Buddy or Group if you are not executing your plan and get back on track as quickly as you can.
5. Stay close to your Success Buddy, group and Inner Circle if you feel stuck or are acting out on your FOS Signals.
6. Track your FOS Signals and get help to stop engaging in those behaviors.
7. Seek the help of professional coach if you're not moving forward.
8. Use meditation, affirmations, slogans, and positive feedback to stay focused and centered.

WORKING THROUGH BROWNOUT AND BLACKOUT PERIODS

Have you ever taken a series of focused actions and reaped few or no results? We all have! When it happens, we feel deflated. Our mood plummets. Typically, we feel discouraged, dejected, depressed and despairing. How can we move forward?

Robert Schuller (1984) advises us to get support and "Keep going!" In his book, *Tough Times Never Last but Tough People Do*, Schuller advises us to stay the course and approach brownouts and blackouts as phases that need to be endured so we can triumph over them.

As Schuller conceives it, a brownout happens when you take many focused actions and get lukewarm results. You've given your project attention through preparation, time, travel, money, networking, and creativity. You do see some results but have little to show for your efforts. Brownout periods are upsetting. You question whether you're on the right track. Enthusiasm and dedication wane.

Brownout periods don't last, but they do diminish our enthusiasm. The psychological and spiritual trick during these times is to continue taking actions until you see more encouraging results. Work closely with your Success Buddy or Group to get the support and encouragement you need to keep moving forward. Borrow their belief in you and in your Vision.

A blackout is when you put in enormous effort, extend yourself fully, and get absolutely no results. Like an energy failure, everything fades to black. Your efforts feel fruitless. Blackouts masquerade as failures or bad decisions and can make you feel as if you're pursuing the wrong career, project or focus.

Do not despair. When you experience a blackout period, the answer is often just around the corner. Lean heavily on your support system; their outside perspective is crucial at this time. Listen to what your supporters say. They will encourage you to hold the course and keep moving in the direction of your Vision.

Brownouts and blackouts are just moments in time where things are in transition. These periods do not predict the future, nor do they invalidate your dream or Vision. They're just part of the success process. They serve a purpose; they are an integral part of moving forward.

Success takes work, and it has its ups and downs. When I'm in a brownout or blackout period, I buckle my seatbelt and prepare for a bumpy ride. The good news is this: I have come through every one of those times better and more successful than when I entered it. You will too!

SHOULD I STAY THE COURSE OR GIVE UP?

Brownout and blackout phases engender the question: "Should I go in another direction or stay the course?" The rule of thumb: Stay the course.

True, there are instances when the job you are pursuing, the career you envision or the business you create is unworkable, and you must let go and move in a different direction. Again, your supporters and Success Buddy or Group can help you assess your situation from objective viewpoints. Take their input into consideration. However, the brownout and blackout periods usually do not signal this kind of change. These periods usually ask us to keep faith and pace with our original idea.

Brownouts and blackouts happen to everyone. They are a natural and organic part of the process, and we must adapt to them. We may need to adjust our Action Plan or get some professional advice, but we don't necessarily need to abandon our dream!

Rather than reflect failure, these periods reflect a transition, reorganization or germination phase. Something could well be brewing in our favor.

Tips for when you are in a brownout or blackout phase:

1. Substitute faith for fear. When you feel discouraged, borrow the faith that others have in you. Lean on their optimism and belief in your goal.
2. Discuss your Action Plan with your Success Buddy or Group.
3. Take suggestions and value new insights.
4. Get feedback from experienced and successful people who work in the arena of your choice. Ask if your Action Plan needs a course correction.

SELF-ACTUALIZATION

Self-actualization happens when you become the best version of your highest self. This is when you live day to day using your gifts, being authentic and achieving your personal best. In your career and creative endeavors, self-actualization comes about when you are firing on all cylinders and operating free from self-sabotage and conflict.

Self-Actualization is a lifetime process. "Process" is the operating word here. Self-Actualization is not a destination. You don't reach self-actualization and stop growing or moving forward. It is a lifetime process of moving forward in service to yourself and the planet. Keep in mind that steady progress is the name of the game. I tell my clients, go slower to go faster. Commit yourself to the journey and to a lifetime of progress not perfection. You will develop the patience, unconditional love and regard for yourself that help you persist. Try it! It really works!

CHAPTER 15

TOOL 5:
DO A FEELING CHECK-IN

What you feel counts. Emotions play a critical role in our daily lives and in the FOS drama. Feelings give us important information about others, what is going on in the environment and whether or not our needs are being met. When it comes to our work and creative endeavors, our feelings can clue us into how we perceive ourselves and how others can inspire feelings of self-acceptance or self-criticism.

Tool 5 encourages you to do regular feeling check-ins and asks you to pay attention to what is going on inside you. When you tune into your feelings and make them conscious, you give yourself the opportunity to be aware of negative feelings such as anger, fear, pain, shame and guilt, and positive feelings such as joy, love, and passion. Important to note is that both positive and negative feelings can trigger self-sabotaging behaviors.

Tool 5 suggests you tune into your feelings. Pay special attention to your anxiety level and become familiar with the warnings anxiety puts inside your head. The explanations and exercises that follow will help you tune into your feelings, assess your anxiety temperature and identify the inner language that emerges when you feel anxious. Here's how:

CHECK IN WITH YOUR FEELINGS

Track your feelings on a daily basis. I recommend carrying a small notebook you can use to record your feelings. Use the feeling chart below to identify what you are feeling. Record your feelings in your notebook for thirty days. I recommend you do a feeling check-in four times a day:

- In the morning when you awake
- In the afternoon
- In the early evening
- Before you go to bed

When you record your feelings in your notebook, write the date, the feeling(s) and the thought attached to the feeling. A word or two, or a simple phrase will do.

If you don't record in real time, record at the end of the day. Think back through your day and write about how you felt. Reflect on what you were feeling and record any thoughts you have about why you were feeling that way. Ask yourself, "Did I know what I wanted and needed?" "Did I get what I wanted and needed?" Positive and negative feelings are related to getting or not getting what we want or need. Study your thought processes. This will increase self-awareness and self-esteem.

TAKE YOUR ANXIETY TEMPERATURE

When we feel safe and relaxed, we feel calm. At these times, it is easy to concentrate, be creative and stay focused. When we feel unsafe or in danger, anxiety appears. Anxiety has physical, cognitive and emotional components. On the physical level, anxiety makes us feel racy, nervous and compulsive inside. It can cause inertia or compel us to do something. On a cognitive level, we have worried thoughts and anticipate negative

The 8 Basic Emotions

THE LARGER FEELING	DIFFERENT FORMS OF THE SAME FEELING	THE GIFT	WHERE IN THE BODY DO YOU FEEL?
Anger	Irritation Annoyance Frustration Rage	Assertiveness Strength Energy Self-Regulation	**ALL OVER BODY** Power Energy
Fear	Anxiety Apprehensive Overwhelmed Threatened	Preservation Wisdom Protection	**STOMACH UPPER CHEST** Suffocation
Pain	Hurt Sad Lonely Rejected	Healing Growth Awareness	**LOWER CHEST HEART** Hurting
Joy	Happy Excited Elated Hopeful	Abundance Happiness Gratitude	**ALL OVER BODY** Lightness
Passion	Enthusiastic Interested Fascinated Strong Desire	Appetite Energy Excitment	**ALL OVER BODY** Energized Recharged Spontaneous
Love	Affection Tenderness Compassion Warmth Respect	Connecttion Life Spirituality	**HEART** Swelling Warmth
Shame	Embarrassed Self-Hate Worthless Inferior	Humility Humanity Self Control	**FACE, NECK, UPPER CHEST** Warmth Feeling Hot Red
Guilt	Wrong Regretful Sorry	Values Amends Self Control	**GUT** Gnawing sensation

Revised and adapted from ©Pia Mellody's *Eight Basic Emotions.*

outcomes. I call this negative futurizing. On the emotional level, anxiety is a form of fear.

The fears FOS generates were described in the early chapters of the book and warrant review here. FOSers fear and/or feel uncomfortable with:

- criticism, disapproval and negative judgment
- anger, jealousy, envy and unfriendly-competitive behavior
- self-doubt and self-esteem issues
- achievement and success
- owning their own creativity and empowerment
- staying right sized

The downside to anxiety is that it has the ability to paralyze us or drive us into impulsive action. Even mild anxiety is uncomfortable enough to trigger us to engage in FOS behaviors. For this reason, it is imperative that we lower anxiety in its earlier stages to diminish its ability to trigger us into self-sabotage.

ASSESS YOUR ANXIETY LEVEL

Tune into your feelings and take your anxiety temperature as soon as you become aware you feel anxious. Follow these steps:

1. Keep your elbow stationary at your side and point your index finger forward. Keep your index finger pointed forward and still. This finger position (no movement) represents a relaxed state where you feel no anxiety, no internal struggle, and no conflict.

NO ANXIETY
(finger is motionless)

2. Next, imagine a time when you felt anxious. Keep your elbow stationary at your side. With your index finger pointed forward, move it up (toward the ceiling) and down (toward the floor) at a pace that matches the anxiety level you're remembering. If you are imagining mild anxiety, move your index finger up and down very slowly. If you are imagining moderate anxiety, move your index finger up and down a little faster. If you are imagining feeling very anxious, move you finger up and down rapidly.

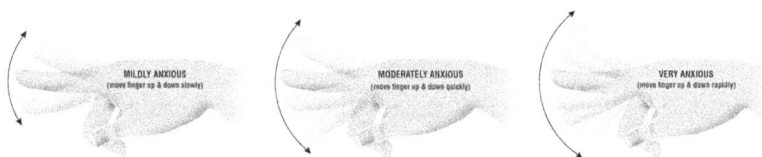

3. Now, come into the present moment. Focus your attention on how you feel now, right this minute. Move your index finger at a pace that matches your internal feeling state. Do you feel relaxed and calm or anxious? Assess and then move your index finger at a pace that matches what you are feeling.

LOWER YOUR ANXIETY

Anxiety is an emotional alert system that says, "You're in danger." Use the following techniques to help you manage your anxiety and understand its message:

- Press the pause button. Take a couple of deep breaths and let each out slowly.
- Take your anxiety temperature.
- Journal about your feelings. Try to write for a few minutes (5–10 is optimal). At the top of the page, write, *I am anxious because* . . . then free associate. Make a bullet list of everything that comes to mind. Often what we think is causing our anxiety is not.

- Contact your Success Buddy or someone from your support group or Inner Circle and make arrangements to share your writing.
- Do a relaxation exercise like this at any time:
  - ☞ Lie down, close your eyes and scan your body from your head to your toes. Identify any areas that are uncomfortable, anxious, or in pain. Send a swirling cooling breath to each area or go to that part of your body and tense your muscles—hold for a few seconds and release. When you are done, breathe in a deep breath and let it slide to the back of your neck, down your spine, pelvis and legs and let it leave through your toes. Take one or two more breaths and let each slide to the back of your neck, down your body and out your toes. Release any worries, concerns, fears and resentments.
- Meditate using a Breathing-Mantra Meditation. Choose the length of time that suits you—5, 10, 15 or 20 minutes—and follow these directions:
  - ☞ Set your timer. Close your eyes and visualize your breath flowing in and out of your nostrils in your mind's eye. When you breathe in, say *So* in your mind, when you breathe out, say *Hum*. Continue to follow your breath using the mantra, *So Hum, So Hum*. You will soon fall into a smooth rhythm of *So Hum, So Hum*. In Sanskrit, this means I am, I am.
- Create a plan with your Success Buddy so you know what to do when you feel anxious. You may have to experiment before you get a plan that works. Keep tweaking your plan until you have one that is successful.

MAKE AN ACTION PLAN TO LOWER YOUR ANXIETY

Make sure you have an action plan in place to lower your anxiety level. Even mild anxiety can interfere with performance and take you off your game. Tim's Action Plan gives you an idea of how to create a set of steps to address anxiety.

Let your Success Buddy know you're anxious and get help with creating your plan. You can also collaborate with members of your Inner Circle. Let others help you.

Sample Action Plan

STEP	ACTION	WHEN
	Tim's Action Plan to Address Anxiety	
1	Push the pause button and breathe. Take my anxiety temperature to assess my level of anxiety. Tell myself, "I'm okay."	As soon as I'm aware I feel anxious
2	Call, text, or email John (my Success Buddy). If he doesn't respond promptly, contact Derick or Shawn. Talk out what's worrying me.	ASAP
3	Lower my anxiety level by doing a relaxation meditation. Bookend with John or support person.	After Step 2
4	Follow the relaxation technique with a mantra meditation for at least five minutes. Bookend with John or support person.	After Step 3
5	Journal as soon as possible even if I only take 2 or 3 minutes.	After Step 4
6	Share my writing with John.	Call and make a time to talk

My Action Plan

EXERCISE: Create your own action plan based on the following steps and actions in the sample below:

STEP	ACTION	WHEN
1	I will push the pause button and breathe; take my anxiety temperature to assess my level of anxiety; tell myself, "I'm okay."	As soon as I'm aware I feel anxious
2	I will call, text, or email _____ (my Success Buddy); if he/she doesn't respond promptly, contact _____; talk out what's worrying me.	ASAP
3	I will lower my anxiety level by doing a relaxation meditation; bookend with someone from my support system.	After Step 2
4	I will follow the relaxation technique with a mantra meditation for at least five minutes; bookend with my Success Buddy or support person.	After Step 3
5	I will journal as soon as possible even if I only take 2 or 3 minutes.	After Step 4
6	I will share my writing with my Success Buddy, Spiritual Partner or someone from my Inner Circle.	Call and make a time to talk

ANXIETY IS A PROBLEM ON THE RISE

Anxiety is not just a problem for FOSers; current statistics show that anxiety is snowballing in the US and globally, as well. In August 2018, Barnes and Noble, the largest book retailer in the US, registered a twenty-five percent jump in book sales on the topic of anxiety. Tim Newman (September 2018) reported on anxiety statistics from the US and 26 other countries showing that anxiety is on the rise globally, with the US leading the way in percentages.

The National Health Service (NHS) estimates that over 40 million Americans suffer from some form of anxiety. When formally diagnosed by a physician or mental health professional, anxiety is labeled as GAD (generalized anxiety disorder). The World Health Organization (WHO) reports that almost 300 million people worldwide have an anxiety disorder.

As a clinician, I find that anxiety is a frequent problem among all age groups—adults, adolescents and children. Therefore, I question whether the stats described are lower than the real numbers.

In addition, anxiety is not a modern emotion. Robert Burton wrote in *The Anatomy of Melancholy* (1621) about a patient described by Hippocrates, which dates back some 2300 years. Hippocrates' narrative of the patient's problem will resonate with anyone who has experienced anxiety in the same way:

> "He dare not come into company for fear he should be misused, disgraced, overshoot himself in gestures or speeches, or be sick; he thinks every man observeth him."

Hippocrates
(CE 460 BC–370 BC)

The description of the patient's problem illustrates that anxiety is a troublesome emotion that arose early in our human history. It was first used to warn us about physical danger. Nowadays, when no tigers or bears or rival clans are coming to get us, it operates as though there were. In the example above, the man feared negative emotional consequences that would lead him to feel shame, humiliation and low self-esteem.

When anxiety operates in this way, it does not serve you and it is not your friend. To come into emotional balance, you need to lower its impact as soon as possible. One way to handle the discomfort is to make friends with your anxiety. Use the suggestions I provided earlier in the chapter. Identify your anxiety. Take your anxiety temperature. Listen for the message it's sending. Get in touch with your worries and fears. If you let it, anxiety will become one of your best teachers. Try it!

IN SUMMARY

Tool 5 suggests you pay attention to your inner life and tune into your feelings. This tool encourages you to:

1) Do a feeling check-in using the feeling chart;

2) Take your anxiety temperature;

3) Lower your anxiety as soon as possible; and

4) Understand anxiety's message.

CHAPTER 16

Tool 6:
Quiet Your Inner Critic

Understanding Your Inner Critic

When you feel ashamed, hopeless, inadequate, or just plain awful about yourself, it's because your Inner Critic is attacking you. The Inner Critic refers to an inner voice (a kind of subpersonality) that judges and demeans us. The Inner Critic is experienced as an internal voice attacking us, saying we are bad, wrong, unworthy, or inferior.

We all have at least one Inner Critic and some of us have more. When an Inner Critic is active, it hammers us with negative messages about our self-worth and performance. Inner Critics poison passion, esteem and self-confidence. To counteract their lethal effect, you need an antidote. The ultimate antidote is self-love, acceptance and confidence in your intuition and ability to take right action. To get there, you need to practice being gentle and loving to yourself.

To develop a new habit and create an inner voice that gives you positive feedback, enlist the help of your Success Buddy, Spiritual Partner and trustworthy supporters in your Inner Circle. They represent a positive presence and a positive voice that will help you counteract the negative messages of your Inner Critic.

Your Inner Critic can do any of the following:

- Evaluate and judge your feelings, behaviors and your core self.
- Tell you what you should and shouldn't do.
- Criticize you for not meeting its expectations or the expectations of people who are important to you.
- Doubt you and tell you that you can't be successful.
- Shame you for who you are.
- Make you feel guilty about things you have done.

Types of Inner Critics

Most people have a number of self-judging Inner Critics who show up at various times. Listen for their voices and how they communicate. These are some of the typical Inner Critics who show up with negative messages:

1. **The Perfectionist:** tries to get you to do everything perfectly. It has very high standards for behavior, performance and production.
2. **The Inner Controller:** tries to control your impulses, desires and behavior. It dampens your ability to be spontaneous.
3. **The Taskmaster:** tries to get you to work hard in order to be successful. It attempts to motivate you by berating you, telling you that you're lazy, stupid or incompetent.
4. **The Underminer:** undermines your self-confidence and self-esteem so you won't take risks and live in your potential.
5. **The Destroyer:** attacks your self-worth. It is deeply shaming and tells you that you shouldn't exist.
6. **The Guilt Tripper:** attacks you for a specific action you took or didn't take. It reprimands you and often "beats you up."
7. **The Approval Seeker:** drives you to behave in a way that will win approval. It compels you to act in a way that will be acceptable to other people.

8. **The Spoiler:** ruins things. It plays havoc with your vision, dreams, ideas and accomplishments. If you have a big win, it devalues it. If you make a small amount of progress, it degrades it. It destroys your *joie de vivre*.

EXERCISE: Name your own Inner Critic.

If you have an Inner Critic that is not discussed above, name and define it here:

1. _____

2. _____

YOU CAN QUIET YOUR INNER CRITICS

First things first. Know your enemy! To quiet your Inner Critic, become familiar with its voice, its message and how it operates. You can begin to engage with your Inner Critic by doing a role play using a technique called *personification*. Personification is when we give a human quality to a feeling, an animal, or an object.

You can know how the device of personification works from animated films. The teapot in *Beauty and the Beast* comes to life as Mrs. Potts. In the animated film, *Inside Out*, eleven-year-old Riley's feelings of joy, sadness, anger, fear and disgust become human and assume separate identities. Each talks and acts like a person.

The movie illustrates how Riley's negative feelings—Anger, Fear and Disgust—push away Joy and get Riley to ignore Sadness. Her emotions give her a hard time in the same way your Inner Critics do.

The exercise described later in the chapter will give you the opportunity to talk *to* and *for* your Inner Critics. The role play allows you to clarify what your Inner Critic is saying and gives you an opportunity to respond.

Let's see how this worked with my client Lori.

Lori

Lori, a 15-year-old, came to me complaining of perfectionism. In the first interview, she said, "Perfectionism is making it hard for me to play soccer. I'm always criticizing myself and it ruins other parts of my life, too."

Her sports history revealed she had been playing soccer since she was nine years old and had always been hard on herself. She described herself as overly perfectionistic, self-critical and vacillating in self-confidence. By the time she saw me, attacking herself was a habit that became so severe, she was in tears after every game and wanted to quit the team. To make matters worse, she had sustained a serious knee injury and felt miserable she wasn't back one hundred percent.

However, the injury had a silver lining. Sitting on the bench gave her a different perspective on practices and games. Watching from the sidelines increased her understanding of technical skills and clarified game strategy. She became smarter about the game. The colleague who referred her agreed that post-injury, Lori's technical skills were better, and she was strategically savvier.

By the time Lori came to see me, she was ready to try anything that might help her feel better. In the initial interview, Lori described her obsessive need to be perfect and devalue herself as a player. We called the coach to get his opinion of her skills and contribution to the team. He said she was an excellent player who had a positive impact on the team effort. "Her biggest problem," he said, "was being too hard on herself and not giving herself enough credit."

As our work progressed, Lori discovered that perfectionism was not her only problem. She identified a number of Inner Critics giving her a hard time, i.e., the Underminer, the Approval Seeker and the Spoiler.

I explained that she needed to quiet her Inner Critics or they would continue to bully and harass her. The next section describes what we did.

LORI GETS READY TO DIALOGUE
WITH HER INNER CRITICS

We set up two chairs (one for Lori and one for me) and then reviewed the list of Inner Critics. Lori identified three that were giving her a hard time: the Perfectionist, the Underminer, and the Approval Seeker. Using different colored markers, she wrote the name of each Inner Critic on a separate piece of paper and what each said to her.

Her papers looked like this:

Perfectionist	"You have to be the best."
	"You have to get 100% on everything."
Underminer	"Everyone else is better than You."
	"You suck!"
	"You're pathetic."
Approval Seeker	"Everyone else thinks you suck."
	"What does the coach (my teammates) think about that?"

Next, we set up three chairs facing us about five feet away. Lori placed one piece of paper describing each of her Inner Critics on the floor in front of each chair. I sat next to Lori to guide the dialogue and then we began the role play.

LORI'S DIALOGUE WITH HER INNER CRITICS

Dr. C: Who do you want to talk to first?

L: The Perfectionist. What do I say?

Dr. C: Say whatever comes to your mind.

L: Why are you telling me to be perfect or it doesn't count?

Dr. C: (Instruction) Go sit in the Perfectionist's chair and answer.

The Perfectionist: I'm only trying to help you be the best and succeed. You can't be successful unless you're perfect.

Dr. C: (Instruction) Now sit in your chair and answer the Perfectionist as Lori.

L: It's not working. You're making me miserable. I can't play the game. I'm crying and I want to quit the team. I can't be perfect all the time. Nobody is perfect all the time.

The Perfectionist: It's my job to push you to be perfect or you won't push yourself to be the best.

Dr. C: (to the Perfectionist): I don't understand. It sounds like you don't think Lori has a good work ethic. Don't you think she has a strong desire to be the best player she can be?

The Perfectionist: Yes, she is a hard worker. I feel it's my job to remind her she won't be successful unless she is perfect. That's why I tell her she has to be the best.

Dr. C: (to the Perfectionist) Are you aware you are upsetting her? (Perfectionist nods a Yes) She feels like she wants to quit soccer. She's in tears off and on the field. She also gets other messages. Do you have helpers?

The Perfectionist: Yes, I do. My buddies are the Underminer and the Approval Seeker. They help me out because I'm limited. I have only one message: "Be perfect or it doesn't count!" They say other things.

Dr. C: (to Lori): Sit in the Underminer's chair and talk for the Underminer.

The Underminer: I'm Lori's Underminer. My job is to chip away at her self-confidence and self-esteem. I tell her everyone is better than her. I say, "you suck" and "you're pathetic."

Dr. C: You are mean and nasty, aren't you?

The Underminer: (smiling) Yes, I am. And I'm good at my job.

Dr. C: I can see that!

L: (to the Underminer) Why me? Why are you bullying me?

The Underminer: Because you're an easy target. You're vulnerable and I can attack you every time you're not perfect.

Dr. C: (to the Approval Seeker) What's your job?

The Approval Seeker: I distract Lori and make her anxious. I get her worried about what people think about her. I say, "They think YOU SUCK!" I distract her mind by getting her to ask, "What is the coach thinking?"

The dialogue here is a sample of what happened when Lori talked to her Inner Critics and talked for them. The illustration below shows the chair set up and where Lori and I sat.

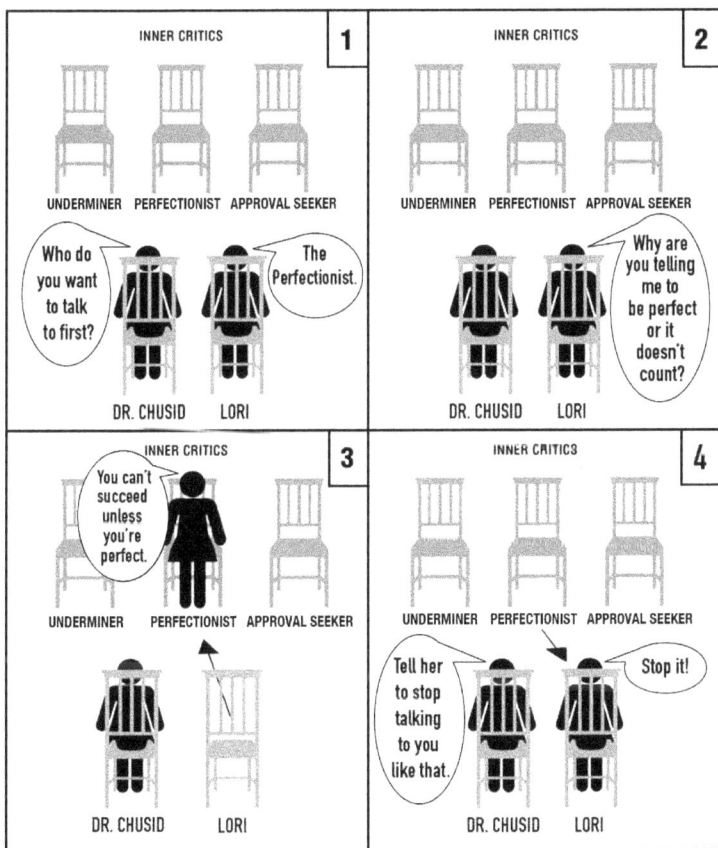

During the role play, Lori's Inner Critics revealed they planned to keep harassing her. In response to their stubborn attitude, she decided to modify the Perfectionist's job and give the Underminer and the Approval Seeker new job assignments. She changed her papers to look like this:

Perfectionist	Modified Job	Support Lori's 100% commitment & effort
Underminer	New Job Assignment. Take the arrogant players who are overconfident down a notch.	Susie & Gabriel
Approval Seeker	New Job Assignment: Go to the players who don't care what anyone thinks.	Jane & Zoe

She reassigned the Underminer and the Approval Seeker to players on the team who could use their expertise. She told both critics to "pack their bags and move out." She sent the Underminer to Susie and Gabriel who are arrogant and overconfident. She imagined the Underminer would take them down a notch. She sent the Approval Seeker to Jane and Zoe, who are too independent and overly self-reliant. Because they don't care about other people's opinions, Lori felt they could use the voice of the Approval Seeker.

This exercise can have an immediate and positive effect. That was true for Lori for a while, but then the Underminer returned to harass her. I include what happened next to give you an idea of what to do if your Inner Critics resist leaving you alone. Lori and I used a number of other techniques to quiet the voices of her Inner Critics. You can try these as well.

When her Underminer raised its ugly head, Lori sent me this text:

> I have been having new problems with the Underminer. Now, even before I touch the ball, it starts telling me that I'm not fast enough and don't have enough skills to win the ball or beat my opponent. It tells me that I can't do it/won't succeed.

In our next session, we discussed the importance of substituting positive messages for negative ones. I asked Lori if she thought it would help her if I recorded positive messages on her iPhone. She liked the idea and wrote down phrases for me to read and record as voice memos on her phone. Here's what I recorded:

> *I'll be thinking of you—I'm right with you on the field—good job, do it again. Have fun! You're doing a great job! You're an outstanding player! You can definitively do this—you are doing this—you have been doing this since you were a kid. I believe in you—you're a great defender—I love watching you play!*

A few days later, she texted this message:

> . . . as for the games this weekend, the tape recordings of your voice seemed to have helped. I did not have as many moments in the game where my critics said negative things to me . . . At least I haven't cried on the field for a while now. Do you think we could make more recordings of your voice for me? I can send you the list of positive phrases I wrote in the small notebook you gave me.

After our initial success. Lori created a list of 32 positive messages in a little book I gave her. They looked like this:

4/10/19	4/23/19
"Stellar job!"	"You've got this!"
"Magnificent skill!"	"You can do it!"
"That was awesome!"	"You will succeed!"
"You're so talented!"	"You will do great!"
"That looks fabulous!"	"You're such a kind/good person!"
"You're so multifaceted!"	"What a talented artist!"
"I wish I could be you!"	"You're so unique!"
"Your art looks so good!"	"We love/support you!"
"You're so smart!"	"You're a great leader!"
"Keep going!"	"I'm so proud of you!"
"You're the best!"	"Your smile is incredible!"
"You're great!"	"You look so good!"
"Great job!"	"You're firing on all cylinders!"
"Fantastic defense!"	"How incredible!"

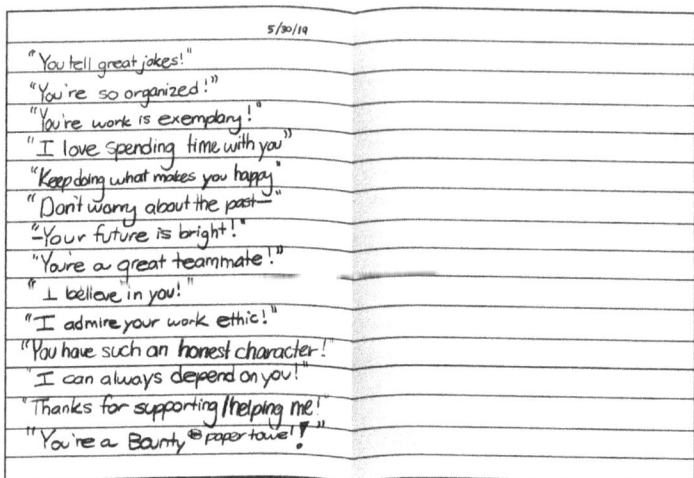

The list was followed by this text message:

> I was also able to make the 2 tracks we already have into loops! So I can play them while I sleep.

In her next session, I read and recorded the 32 messages she created in groups of eight. She looped them so she could hear them repeatedly. The second set of recordings helped enormously and she said her Inner Critics took a secondary place in her repertoire. Eight weeks later, we achieved a number of other breakthroughs and Lori began to hear the positive messages of her Inner Supporters.

EXERCISE: Dialogue with Your Inner Critics

When you're ready, dialogue with your Inner Critics by duplicating what Lori and I did. Enlist your Success Buddy, Spiritual Partner or someone from your Inner Circle to help.

Remember, in this role play you speak for yourself and for your Inner Critic. The exercise works best if you say what comes to mind spontaneously. If you become a curious, non-judgmental observer, what you learn

Inner Critics-Inner Supporters

INNER CRITIC	THE INNER CRITIC'S MESSAGE	TRUSTWORTHY SUPPORTER	INNER SUPPORTER'S MESSAGE
The Perfectionist	• You must do everything perfectly. • You can't make mistakes.	**The Coach**	• You always give your best effort and strive for accuracy. • Keep practicing. • Good job, do it again!
The Inner Controller	• You can't think, feel or do that.	**The Acceptor**	• You're entitled to your thoughts and feelings. • Do what's in your best interest. • Be spontaneous!
The Taskmaster	• Work harder- do more!	**The Inspired Worker**	• You have a great work ethic. • You're a hard worker. • You're creative and skilled
The Underminer	• You're a loser. • Nothing you do counts.	**The Encourager**	• You're gifted and talented. • You have vision. • Take risks – keep going!
The Destroyer	• Everyone's better than you.	**The Cheerleader**	• You can achieve whatever you want.
The Guilt Tripper	• Your mistake Is irreversible. • You should have done (or said) something else.	**The Soother**	• A mistake is an opportunity to learn. • It's just a mistake, you can do something different next time.
The Approval Seeker	• What do others think of me? • Disapproval feels unsafe.	**The Self-Approver**	• I approve of myself. • I'm doing a good job. • I'm creative and worthwhile. • I love the way I'm approaching this.

can be surprisingly powerful and enlightening. I have dialogued with my Inner Critics many times and facilitated this with hundreds of clients. I am always amazed at the wealth of information revealed.

Begin by reading the types of Inner Critics from the Inner Critics – Inner Supporters chart. Identify your Inner Critics. Write the name of each Inner Critic on a separate piece of paper and the message each conveys. Arrange the room with two chairs (or pillows)—one for you and one for your buddy. Next, place an empty chair for each Inner Critic facing you and your buddy. Place the paper naming each Inner Critic on the floor in front of an empty chair. Sit next to your buddy and begin the dialogue.

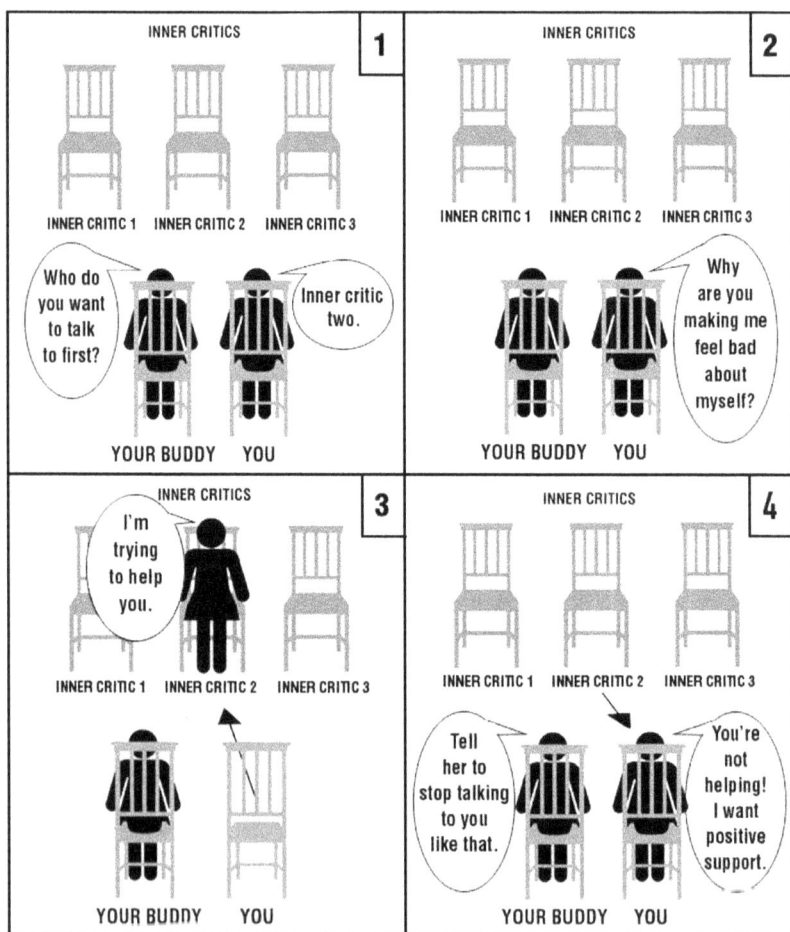

Once you have completed your dialogue, discuss what you learned with the person who helped you. Create an Action Plan with your Success Buddy to address the steps you will take when your Inner Critics talk to you. Journal about your experience.

EXERCISE: Dialogue with Your Inner Supporters

Once you have quieted your Inner Critics, you need to adopt supportive inner voices that inspire, encourage, and empower you. The chart on the preceding page lists Inner Supporters and the positive messages they convey. Choose the Inner Supporters you need and create a dialogue with them. Develop a daily practice of talking with your Inner Supporters. Five to ten minutes a day is all it takes. If you practice, the voices of your Inner Supporters will become louder and stronger than your Inner Critics.

In Summary

Tool 6 shows you how to identify and dialogue with your Inner Critics so you can quiet their voices. This tool also teaches you how to substitute the negative messages of your Inner Critics for positive ones from your Inner Supporters.

CHAPTER 17

TOOL 7:
CLARIFY YOUR VISION

"A journey of a thousand miles begins with a single step."

Lao-tzu, Chinese philosopher
(CE 604 BCE–531 BCE)
The Way of Lao-tzu

Tool 7 will help you clarify your Vision and commit to your short- and long-term goals so you can move toward doing work you love. Vision work includes making a plan to improve your work life *now*, tuning into your passion, gaining clarity about your purpose, converting your passion into work you love, and creating an Action Plan that moves you incrementally toward your goals.

VISION WORK BEGINS WHERE YOU ARE

Scholars say a more accurate translation of the quote from Lao-tzu (*A journey of a thousand miles begins with a single step*) would be "The journey of a thousand miles begins beneath one's feet." Likewise, Vision work begins where you are.

Studying Lao-tzu's writings (5th–6th Century BCE), we find he regarded action as significant and something that arises naturally from stillness. Keeping this in mind, Michael Moncur (2004) suggested that an even more accurate translation of the above quote would be "Even the longest journey must begin from where you stand."

Vision Work Begins Here

Keeping this in mind—let's begin from where you are right now. First, be gentle with yourself. Second, review your answers on the Vision Issue Checklist from Chapter 4. Third, focus on the specific Vision issue that applies to you. Fourth, keeping in mind your Vision issue, answer the questions below:

1. Do I love what I do?
2. Am I happy in my work environment?
3. Is it time to make a change?
4. What is my work/career goal?
5. Have I created an Action Plan to help me accomplish my goal?

To move forward in your work life, you must understand what is making you unhappy and what is keeping you stuck. Spiritual wisdom teaches us that feeling discontent, unhappy or confused means we are out of balance emotionally and spiritually. Unhappiness is a message that something needs changing. Pay attention to your pain and discomfort.

Tool 7 encourages you to unravel why you are stuck and unhappy. Like any good detective, you must follow the evidence. Each piece of evidence will give you insights.

Think about the statements below and check the ones that feel true.

- ❑ I am unhappy because I'm confused about my Vision.
- ❑ I am unable to choose among multiple Visions.
- ❑ I am unable to manifest a very clear Vision.

❑   I am underearning.

❑   I am underachieving.

❑   I am performing inconsistently.

❑   I am unable to make a career change or transition, or afraid to do what I want to do.

❑   I am using my job or career to medicate my feelings or run away from my life.

❑   I am not satisfied with my present level of achievement.

❑   I am feeling uncomfortable, anxious or frightened being at the top of my field.

EXERCISES

CLARIFY YOUR VISION WORK BY FOLLOWING THE SUGGESTIONS BELOW:

A.   Meditate for ten minutes, then write your answers to the questions listed below.

- Are my feet planted in my right livelihood?
- Are my feet pointed in the direction of my passion?
- Are my feet "dancing" to what I love to do?
- Are my feet following my bliss?
- What is my definition of blissful work?
- What comes to your mind when you think of the phrase: *Do what you love and the money will follow!*?

B.   Choose the Vision issue that applies to you and write ten minutes a day for four weeks about the questions that apply to your issue. Feel free to add your own questions. As you complete each week of writing, share it with your Success Buddy.

1.   I have a clear Vision but have difficulty working on it consistently.

WEEK 1: What is my Vision? How much of my Vision am I manifesting?

WEEK 2: What FOS Signals do I engage in that block me from living my Vision fully?

WEEK 3: What would my work life be like if I were using my full potential?

WEEK 4: When I think about living my Vision, do I start to feel anxious and slip into FOS beliefs, attitudes and feelings?

2. I have trouble knowing or getting in touch with my Vision; my Vision remains unclear.

WEEK 1: What makes me happy? What things am I passionate about? (List everything you love, i.e., Jell-O, walking, reading, socializing, being alone, etc. Then sort the list into categories: career skills, fun, recreational, social, personal, etc.)

WEEK 2: What jobs, careers, or creative endeavors feel like fun?

WEEK 3: What do I think has kept me from creating or knowing my Vision?

WEEK 4: Did anyone discourage me from my dream?

3. I am confused about my Vision.

WEEK 1: Why am I confused? What is my definition of "a Vision"?

WEEK 2: Was there a time I had a dream, Vision or goal?

WEEK 3: How will my life change if I am clear about my Vision?

WEEK 4: What is the payoff to staying confused?

4. I have competing Visions. I never decide on my focus; I am not sure what I am best at and I like a number of things.

WEEK 1: Do I have more than one Vision or passion? (List them, and what appeals to you about each).

WEEK 2: If I choose one Vision and commit to it, how will I feel and what do I imagine will happen?

WEEK 3: How do I feel day-to-day, minute-by-minute, focusing on a number of things?

WEEK 4: Imagine and write about living a blissful work life for each Vision. Describe in detail what your life would be if you lived this way.

CREATE A VISION MAP

A Vision map is a powerful tool. It is a visual representation of how you want your work life to be. When you create a Vision map, you put a prescription into the universe for your career and creative life.

Below are two Vision Map templates. The first incorporates your personal life with your work life; the second focuses solely on your career. Note that in each Vision map, your spiritual life is the center of the board: everything else is arranged around it.

Vision mapping can help you manifest your career goals. It has the potential to be magical in its process and result, if you let your unconscious and conscious mind help you. The unconscious has an uncanny way of choosing the right things.

To embark on the Vision map journey, thumb through magazines, newspapers, books, your picture collection and personal memorabilia. Choose pictures, words, and phrases that call to you. You don't have to understand why you chose a particular picture, word or phrase. Your unconscious mind will be your helper. You may want to create a small drawing or write words or phrases on your Vision map. Do it! Have faith that your unconscious is helping you sculpt your future.

Note that each Vision map template contains categories, areas of your life. The personal life and career template lists love and family relationships/sex and romance, personal life and growth, friendships/social, career, and travel. The career Vision map has only one category: career.

Work with your Vision map by arranging the pictures, words and phrases you've collected, drawn or written on the board. Use a presentation board that is 11" x 14" or bigger. You may want to frame it and hang it somewhere in your home or office, so be conscious of its size. When you're satisfied with the placement of all your pictures, words, phrases and drawings, tape or glue them on.

VISION MAP OF MY PERSONAL LIFE AND CAREER

Love & Family Relationships
Romance and Sex

Personal Life & Growth

My Spiritual Life

Travel

Career

Friendships/
Social

This map should reflect a balance between your personal life and work life.

VISION MAP OF MY CAREER

This map should reflect just your career Vision.

Career

Career

Career

My Spiritual Life

Career

Career

It can reflect a short-term or long-term work Vision.

EXAMPLE OF AN ACTUAL VISION MAP

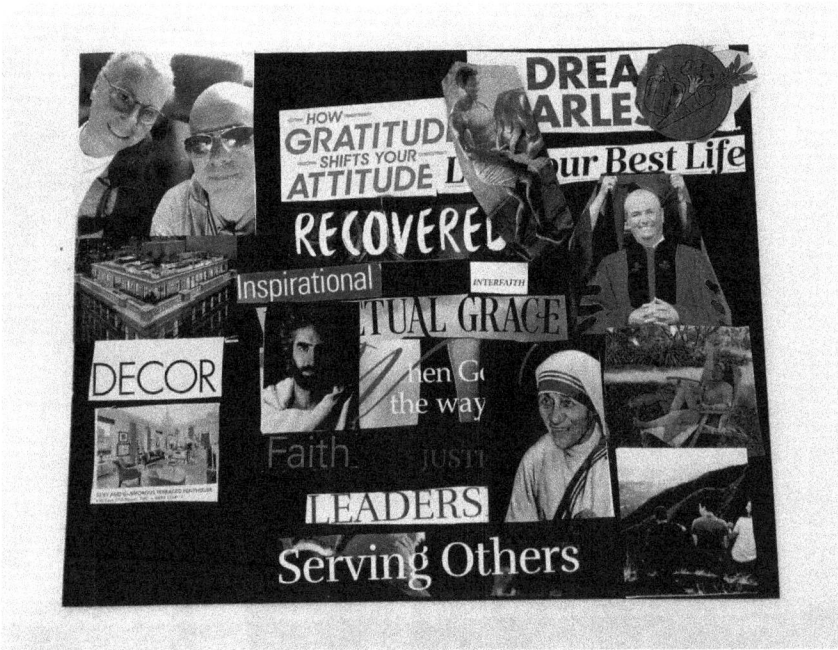

THE MAGIC OF THE VISION MAP

Vision maps are magical! I have seen miracles happen for clients and friends who create Vision maps. Here is just one example: Sara, a friend of mine, is a talented singer, songwriter, and performer. She left the world of finance to perform and was struggling to move her career to a more visible and lucrative level. Her husband was very supportive and encouraging. He helped her self-produce a music CD and filled in as her tech guy at performances. Sara wasn't making money. She had difficulty booking small venue cabaret performances, and larger stage performances were out of the question. She was also having no luck with her auditions for Broadway musicals. Disappointed but willing to try new things, Sara took a Vision map workshop with a friend of ours.

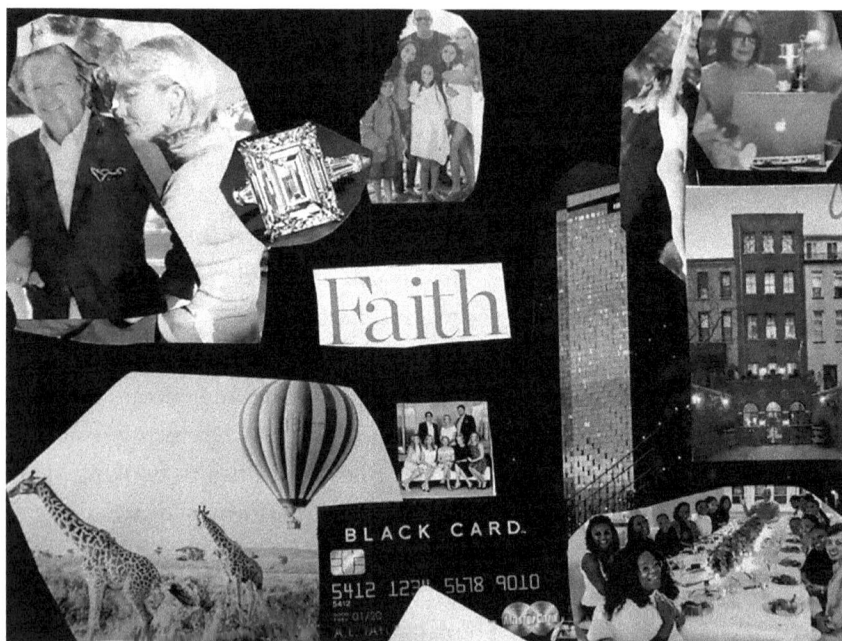

She used a Vision map template similar to the personal and career templates in this chapter. In the career section, she pasted a theatre marquee with the phrase "On Broadway." In her family and love relationship section, she pasted a picture of an apartment building with flowers in front, a parking lot across the street and a picture of a Bosch stackable washer/dryer with red buttons. When she shared her Vision map with me, I questioned the pictures of the building and Bosch washer/dryer. "What is this? And this?" I asked. She said, "I don't know. I just liked the pictures, so I put them there."

A year and a half later, one of the lead actresses in a Broadway musical got pregnant and had to leave the show. Sara booked the job for six months and then went on the road with the touring company for the next year and a half. Next, she and her husband decided they were tired of living in cramped quarters in New York City and began looking for an apartment outside of Manhattan. One afternoon, she called me, excited beyond belief. "Judith, you're not going to believe where I am and what I'm looking at! Remember my Vision map and the photo of a building with flowers and a parking lot I pasted on it?"

"Of course!" I replied.

"Well, I'm standing in front of a building right now and it looks just like that. Dan and I just looked at a loft apartment and we're going to buy it. And, guess what?"

"What?"

"I asked the realtor what was behind these closed louver doors and she said, 'Take a peek!' Judith, it's the Bosch washer/dryer with the red buttons."

Now many years later, I have produced my own Vision maps and seen hundreds more crafted by clients and workshop participants. The results are impressive and illustrate that Vision mapping can be a powerful tool and that letting the unconscious lead the way in doing Vision work is important. Trust what you choose to put on your Vision map. Have faith in the process. I think you will be pleasantly surprised to see that your Vision map can manifest in unexpected ways and move you in the direction of your dreams. Try it!

CHAPTER 18

Tool 8:
Track and Manage
Your FOS Signals

The purpose of Tool 8 is to heighten your awareness and gain more clarity about your FOS behaviors. When you track your FOS Signals, you become conscious of when and how you engage in behaviors that do not serve your Vision and goals.

Get Clear

To heighten your **awareness** and **clarity**, answer these questions:

- Do I have a pattern of interrupting my momentum? If your answer is "Yes," what pattern have you noticed?
- When am I likely to employ an FOS Signal? (Make a trigger list.)
- What feeling or emotional reaction fostered this Signal? (Use the Feeling Chart.)
- What's the payoff? (What do I gain by engaging in this behavior?)

The Trigger List

A trigger list is a list of incidents that happened before you have an emotion and before you engage in an FOS Signal. If you study each experience you will see what triggered you to use an FOS Signal. The sample list below will give you an idea about how to study triggers. Look it over and then make a list of your own.

ADRIENNE'S SAMPLE TRIGGER LIST

What happened?	I did not send my portfolio to Jane Smith at the Smith Gallery.
What FOS Signal(s) was used?	**Procrastination**
What triggered the incident?	I met Jane at the MoMA reception. She asked to see samples of my work, which I had on my phone. She liked my work and requested I send my portfolio to her assistant and make an appointment to come into the gallery for a meeting.
What feelings were triggered?	**Fear**
When did it happen?	Saturday, April 8, 2017
How did the incident come about?	I was introduced to Jane by my friend Peter, who owns a gallery in Chelsea.
What is the outcome?	It's June 2017 and I haven't sent my portfolio or set up an appointment.

Tune into Your Feeling(s)

FOS Signals are driven by feelings. Use the Eight Basic Emotions chart (Chapter 15: Tool 5: Check in with your Feelings) to identify your feelings. Once you're in the habit of identifying your feelings, it will be easier to understand what drives your FOS Signals.

What's the Payoff?

FOS Signals serve you and have a purpose—a payoff. The payoff is what you gain by engaging in FOS behaviors repeatedly. In Adrienne's example above, her immediate payoff is avoidance. Adrienne can ignore and bury her fear and avoid facing her feelings of inadequacy.

Benefits of Tracking FOS Signals

When you track your FOS Signals, you give yourself the opportunity to *observe* and *clarify* what you are doing. This helps you practice the first two stages of the 5As, Awareness and Acceptance.

The best attitude you can have when tracking your FOS Signals is to stay curious and nonjudgmental. Become a compassionate witness to your own process. Observe with curiosity and kindness.

Remember, it's counterproductive to criticize and judge yourself. The goal of this tool is to provide you with a simple and precise way of showing yourself how, when, why and under what circumstances you engage in behaviors that don't serve you or further your goals. Let's look at John.

JOHN

John, a talented teacher with years of experience, was promoted to curriculum coordinator for the fifth grade in his school district. Among his responsibilities was tracking how the teachers implemented the school curriculum and recorded students' progress. He had to produce a quarterly report.

After turning in two reports late, John engaged my help to overcome his fear and procrastination. In spite of being late, John's first report was well-received. However, positive feedback from his boss (the superintendent of the school district) did not encourage John to produce the second report on time. Feeling self-doubt and a lack of confidence, he felt overwhelmed and confused when he had to approach writing the report.

Initially, John thought he could lower his anxiety by meeting with the superintendent after completing his first report. That meeting went well. They clarified content and discussed what the superintendent liked and disliked about John's predecessor's reports. John asked how he could improve upon his own report and the superintendent responded, "Your report is good. Keep doing what you're doing."

That meeting did not resolve John's problem. He continued to act out FOS Signals: negative self-talk, procrastination and holding back in fear. He handed in his second report late and received a warning from the superintendent. He would be removed as curriculum coordinator if the third-quarter report was late.

In his first coaching session, John presented his issues. Assessing his work history, we concluded he devalued his experience and expertise. He said he was shocked that he had been given this promotion. John's reaction did not match his work history. Over the years, he was recognized by his peers and the school administration as a successful and effective teacher, a natural leader and creative thinker. He was respected and liked by his teaching colleagues.

In service of producing his third report on time, he tracked his FOS Signals. The chart below shows John's FOS behaviors, and the commentary illustrates how the FOS categories of fear, self-esteem and negative self-talk caused problems.

JOHN'S FOS SIGNALS CHART

FOS Signal & Category	Procrastination (Fears)
	I resist asking for or accepting help **(Fears)**
Why am I using this signal? **(If you don't know, guess)**	To rationalize why I can't do the report. I'm not experienced enough to do a good job. (Self-Esteem Issues: John is devaluing his talents) I'm not sure how to structure the report or what info to add or delete. The report is due December 15th and I feel frozen. Don't know how to organize the data I have or what commentary to make. I don't want to ask anyone for more help because they'll think less of me. (Fear & Negative Self-Talk)
When—How Often? **(Report due December 15th)**	December 1–14 Daily
My Thoughts **(Write your thought and name the FOS category it falls under)**	I don't think I can pull this off and write a good report. (Self-Esteem Issues & Negative Self-Talk) I'm supposed to know how to do this. Everyone will think I don't know how to do my job if I ask for more help. (Negative Self-Talk) I should never have agreed to be the coordinator. It's obvious that I can't handle this.

The friend who referred John for coaching became his Success Buddy and reviewed John's FOS Signals with him. In the FOS Signal and category, John noted he used procrastination from the Fears category to avoid doing the report.

In the row for "Why Am I Using This Signal," John writes what comes to his mind. In the row, "When and How Often?" John records the frequency and, in the last row, John records his thoughts. Notice the FOS Signal procrastination has helpers:

- Procrastination Helper #1: *I'm supposed to know how to do this!* and *Everyone will think I don't know how to do my job if I ask for help.* Both of these statements can be categorized as *Self-Esteem Issues* and *Negative Self-Talk.* For sure, both thoughts undermine his confidence and reinforce procrastination.
- Procrastination Helper #2: *I don't think I can pull this off and write a good report.* This thought can be translated into the FOS Signals, *I undervalue my skills* and *I am haunted by self-doubt* from the Self-Esteem Issues category.

John's problem with procrastination illustrates an important phenomenon: Like the Inner Critics, FOS Signals do not work alone. They collaborate! When they do, they create a powerful resistance to success and join forces to become more powerful. Luckily for us, without each other, FOS Signals are pretty much ineffective. Rendering one ineffective helps to level its companion signals. That's why it's so important to track and manage each FOS Signal.

SUCCESS BUDDY EXERCISE

FOS Signals Tracking Chart

EXERCISE: Create a chart to track your FOS Signals with your Success Buddy using the categories below:

- FOS Signal (Put FOS Category in parentheses)
- Why am I using this signal? (Don't know? Guess!)
- When—How Often?
- My Thoughts

Tool 8: Track and Manage Your FOS Signals

Keep in mind that FOS Signals were designed by your unconscious to protect you from the dangers of success. Think about these questions:

- What is so dangerous about achieving my goal?
- Why is success scary?
- What prevents me from being successful on a reliable and consistent basis?

Discover the answers by fishing around for the answers. Take guesses. Use your imagination. Become a psychological detective. I promise, you will make discoveries and gain insight into how FOS serves you.

How to Track and Level Your FOS Signals

1. List your FOS Signals in the FOS Signals Tracking Chart.
2. Put a (✓) check next to each FOS Signal you engage in.
3. Take a daily inventory for seven days. At the end of each day, list the FOS Signals you engaged in.
4. Create an Action Plan. Use the first four of the 5As to make a beginning. Hold yourself accountable by calling, texting or emailing your Success Buddy or Success Group with your plan. Follow the example below:

FOS Signal	**Self-Esteem Issues**
	I need external validation to feel okay.
Action Plan	I will track how many times a day I want someone to praise me and how many times a day I think that money, status or material possessions will make me feel okay.
Which of the 5As am I practicing?	**Awareness** (I need external validation to feel okay.)
	Acceptance (There are many examples of this in my daily life. For today, I accept this is me.)

FOS Signal	**Fears**
	I procrastinate.
Action Plan	I will create a daily task list in priority order. I will bookend when I begin and finish each task. I also will do my best to be realistic.
Which of the 5As am I practicing?	**Action** • Creating task list. • Put in priority order. • Bookend w/my Success Buddy by phone or text.
FOS Signal	**Negative Self-Talk**
	I tell myself, "You'll never make it at this job."
Action Plan	I'll change my inner language to "I can be successful in this job." I'll create an affirmation to act as the antidote: "I have the talent and ability to be successful at this job."
Which of the 5As am I practicing?	**Action** • Call my Success Buddy and get compassionate feedback. • Change my inner language and how I talk to myself. I am way too critical.

Share with your Success Buddy or Success Group about how you acted out on your FOS Signals.

Tracking Works

Tracking your FOS Signals helps you know yourself better. When you compassionately observe the myriad behaviors employed when you are afraid, and become more conscious of how fear drives self-sabotage, you will develop the ability to practice new behaviors and get support to take action *while* you are afraid. Before you know it, you will be able to feel the fear and take action anyway. This is how we neutralize self-sabotage.

CHAPTER 19

TOOL 9:
CREATE AN ACTION PLAN

GETTING INTO ACTION

Tool 9 helps you create a solid Action Plan and be accountable. Using Tool 9 is a fierce action step. This tool helps you *declare* and *do*. Tool 9 helps you understand that a Vision, a dream or a plan without action, is an illusion. You must create an Action Plan and stick to it to achieve your goals.

The best approach is to create a 30-day Action Plan with your Success Buddy. Your Action Plan should include short- and long-term goals and six actionable items.

Be careful not to over-plan or over-promise results. Your Action Plan needs to be realistic in scope and aligned with your ability to complete it. Take time restraints into consideration and respect the commitments you already have. Your Success Buddy can help you create a plan that is sensible and represents who you are.

Accountability

Once you create a plan, you must become accountable for executing each action. This brings you to the fourth stage of the 5As: Accountability.

Your relationship with your Success Buddy is the key to practicing accountability. In your weekly meeting together, report the actions you took and your progress. Be honest and report If you have resistance to executing your plan. If you do, review the FOS Signals that are blocking you from moving forward.

When you are in the Accountability stage, it is best to review the FOS Signals list weekly and identify those that are active. Share with your Success Buddy any feelings, thoughts, attitudes or beliefs that might interfere with your Action Plan or interrupt your momentum. Be authentic and genuine. Be transparent!

Two Types of Action Plans

An action plan is a set of specific actions that will move you incrementally toward your goal. To make progress and head in the direction of your vision, it is important to create an action plan that will help you get what you want.

Action Plans are for Vision work, work goals or both. Tool 9 suggests two types of action plans: Type 1: The Vision Action Plan and Type 2: The Career Action Plan.

Work with your Success Buddy. Use one action plan at a time. First, address Vision issues. Decide if you need to create or clarify, upgrade or recommit to your Vision. If Vision work is called for, use The Vision Action Plan provided in this chapter to move your vision work forward.

Second, use the Career Action Plan when you are ready to take work related actions and when you are prepared to tackle any of the manifestations of FOS we have discussed—underearning, underachieving, inconsistent performance, inability to meet your entrepreneurial goals, workaholism and Sabotage at the Top.

Tool 9: Create an Action Plan

How will you know you are ready to tackle your problem? You will know when you can no longer tolerate repeating and recycling old solutions. You will know you are ready when you feel you must do something different and are one hundred percent committed to taking constructive actions on a reliable and consistent basis.

A solid Career Action Plan will get you into action. You'll feel better about yourself and more hopeful. Taking reliable and consistent action is the key to moving from one stage of the success ladder to the next. A focused Career Action Plan can help you upgrade from a "C" or "D" job (jobs that are not good for you) to a B-Job; transition to a different position, job or career; or move to a better B-Job when your current job stops serving your needs. And ultimately, a focused Career Action Plan will help you move to the top of your game.

Design a plan with your Success Buddy that is *doable*. Create actions that move you forward. Do not let fear stand in your way. Lower your anxiety by breaking down your actions into small steps—tiny steps if necessary. The point is this: keep moving forward, even if you go slowly and use small baby steps. It's better to be engaged in small actions consistently and reliably than to live in procrastination and paralysis.

And keep this in the forefront of your mind: *The foundation of success is action*. Nothing, absolutely nothing, gets accomplished with inertia.

TYPE 1: THE VISION ACTION PLAN

Review the importance of taking Action discussed in Chapter 14 (Tool 4: Practice the 5As). Give yourself permission to update your current Vision, create a new Vision or make a plan to solve any Vision issues you have. Work with your Success Buddy using the Vision Action Plan provided in this chapter. A good Vision Action Plan will help you:

- Create short-term goals.
- Create six actions to accomplish in thirty days.
- Create a wish list.
- Create long-term plans for one, two or five years.

Work with your Success Buddy and support people to develop actions that build from the inside—from your passion. Use the Brainstorming Worksheet to create a list of ideas about converting your passion into career actions. Use the tools of free association, guessing, trying new ideas on for size and collaborative problem solving. By collaborating with your Success Buddy, Spiritual Partner, or someone from your Inner Circle, you give yourself the best opportunity to unlock, clarify or tweak your Vision. Use the Vision Action Plan provided below to create six actions that will move you forward.

If you're still confused about your Vision or still have not created a clear Vision, go back to Chapter 4 (Vision Issues) and review your responses on the Vision Issue Checklist. If you are blocked in this area, focus on brainstorming. Remember, it is impossible to create work you love if you can't identify your passion and convert your passion into action.

THE VISION ACTION PLAN

Brainstorm on a separate worksheet (provided on the next page), whiteboard, or whatever's comfortable for you. Use the Vision Action Plan to record your short- and long-term goals, actions and wish list.

Review the Vision exercises from Chapter 17: Tool 7: Clarify Your Vision. Share your thoughts and writing with your Success Buddy, Group, or anyone from your Inner Circle.

EXERCISE: Help clarify your Vision.

Write for ten minutes a day for the first five days. If you are writing reliably and consistently for the first five days, you can increase your writing time to fifteen minutes for the next five days. Then, if you are writing for fifteen minutes a day reliably and consistently, you can increase to twenty minutes a day.

Tool 9: Create an Action Plan

Vision Action Plan

Today's Date: _____

CHOOSE YOUR WORK:
• tuning into my passion • enlarging my vision • changing/tweaking my vision
• recommitting to my vision

I am working on _____

GOALS: In the space below, list 3 short-term and 3 long-term goals.

Short-Term Goals	Long-Term Goals
1.	1.
2.	2.
3.	3.

30-DAY ACTION LIST: List 6 actions that will support you in moving toward your goal in the next month.

Action:	Complete by:
1.	1.
2.	2.
3.	3.
4.	4.
5.	5.
6.	6.

WISH LIST List 3 things you want to manifest in the next year and 3 wishes for the years to come

1.	1.
2.	2.
3.	3.

Weekly Meeting Plan with Success Buddy
Day: _____ Time: _____
How _____ (In-Person or By Phone or Internet)

© Judith F. Chusid, Ph.D. 2019 - Success Is An Inside Job©

FOR PEOPLE HAVING DIFFICULTY
TUNING INTO THEIR PASSION

WEEK 1: Ask yourself these questions: What makes me happy? What am I passionate about? Make a complete list of the things that make you happy. Include everything, i.e., vanilla ice cream, bubble baths, skipping in the street, etc. List things you feel passionate about. Share with your Success Buddy, Success Group and Spiritual Partner.

WEEK 2: Sort the list of what makes you happy into the following categories: personal; hobby; just because; recreational; things that could be work-related. Ask yourself what job, career or creative endeavor might match my passion list? What job feels like fun? Share with your Success Buddy, Success Group and Spiritual Partner.

WEEK 3: Take your passion and create the ideal job. Write a job description. Let your imagination go wild. Do not judge yourself even if all you can think of is reading or watching TV, movies or plays. Share with your Success Buddy, Success Group and Spiritual Partner.

WEEK 4: Did anyone discourage you from your dream? If yes, who and when? If no, what happened to the passion you came into this world with? Share with your Success Buddy, Success Group and Spiritual Partner.

FOR PEOPLE WITH A CLEAR VISION
BUT AFRAID TO "GO FOR IT"

WEEK 1: List all your fears. Ransack your memory and trace their origin. Did anyone significant discourage you or give you the message your Vision was unrealistic? Share with your Success Buddy, Success Group and Spiritual Partner.

WEEK 2: Ask yourself, "What FOS Signals are blocking me from living my Vision?" Discuss exactly how the FOS Signals interfere with your progress and how they keep you from getting to the top of your game. Share with your Success Buddy, Success Group and Spiritual Partner.

WEEK 3: Ask yourself, "What solutions have I tried?" and "Why haven't they worked?" Interview your close family members, friends and trusted colleagues to get their feedback. How do they perceive you? Are they aware of your Vision problem? Share with your Success Buddy, Success Group and Spiritual Partner.

WEEK 4: Ask yourself, "Have I continued to take actions that don't work?" If your answer is yes, ask yourself: "Why am I recycling actions that do not work?" If an attitude, belief, behavior or action doesn't work, it is not a solution. Ponder these questions: "What's the payoff?" and "What other actions can I take to overcome my FOS?" Share with your Success Buddy, Success Group and Spiritual Partner.

FOR PEOPLE WHO HAVE A CLEAR VISION BUT AREN'T LIVING IT CONSISTENTLY

WEEK 1: Write about your passion. When did you first tune into your passion? How did you convert your Vision into work you love? Write the answers to these questions: "How much of my Vision am I living?" and "Which FOS Signals block me from living my Vision?" Share with your Success Buddy, Success Group and Spiritual Partner.

WEEK 2: Write about what your work life would be if you were working at full potential. Share with your Success Buddy, Success Group and Spiritual Partner.

WEEK 3: Imagine you are living your Vision. What concerns, worries, anxieties or dangers would you have? Find the relationship between your concerns and the FOS Signals you employ. Share with your Success Buddy, Success Group and Spiritual Partner.

WEEK 4: What lies between your fears and your dream? Ask: "If I knew I couldn't fail, what would I do right now?" Share with your Success Buddy, Success Group and Spiritual Partner.

FOR PEOPLE CONFUSED ABOUT THEIR VISION

WEEK 1: Write about confusion. Write the answers to these questions: "Why am I confused?" and "Do I have more than one Vision or passion?" and "Was there a time I had a dream, Vision or goal?" Share with your Success Buddy, Success Group and Spiritual Partner.

WEEK 2: Write about your history of confusion. Answer: "What is my earliest memory of being confused? How long have I been confused? How does my confusion show up? Was there a time I wasn't confused? Did someone significant interfere with my Vision?" Share with your Success Buddy, Success Group and Spiritual Partner.

WEEK 3: Ask yourself: "How many things have I tried in order to solve my Vision problem? Have they worked? Why not?" and "How will my life change if I am clear about my Vision?" Share with your Success Buddy, Success Group and Spiritual Partner.

WEEK 4: What is the payoff to staying confused? Do not shy away from this question. While it may be hard to imagine, there is a payoff for remaining stuck. Find your personal payoff now. The answer will help you move forward. Share with your Success Buddy, Success Group and Spiritual Partner.

Brainstorming Vision Ideas

Brainstorm using the worksheet on the next page, a whiteboard, or whatever feels comfortable for you.

Do the exercises and follow the directions on the Brainstorming Worksheet. If you journal and brainstorm on a regular basis, ideas will start flowing and little by little you will begin to solve your vision issue.

Type 2: The Career Action Plan

Use the Career Action Plan (Chapter 14: Tool 4: Practice the 5As) to work on your FOS issues, enhance your work performance, move to a higher level, change jobs or transition into another career.

A sound Action Plan is a good idea for everyone. For FOSers, it can help you stop acting out on your FOS Signals and help you convert fear into faith, procrastination into action, and negative self-talk into a positive and encouraging inner dialogue.

Your Action Plan will help you:

- Create manageable steps to improve your work performance.
- Develop a strategy to ask for a raise or promotion.
- Identify the FOS Signals preventing you from climbing the corporate ladder or moving forward in your entrepreneurial endeavors.
- Make a career change or transition.
- Identify FOS Signals that might be preventing you from reaching top performance.

CREATE POSSIBILITIES

Make sure you focus on creating short- and long-term goals and sculpting a realistic action plan. A 30-day action plan that includes four to six focused actions is usually very realistic and doable. If you complete your action list early, you can always create a new set of actions.

199

BRAINSTORMING WORKSHEET

Today's Date: _____

Choose your Vision issue:
• tuning into my passion • clarifying my vision • recommitting to my vision
• enlarging my vision • changing or tweaking my vision

I have difficulty: ___ _____

WRITE A BRIEF DESCRIPTION OF YOUR VISION ISSUE:

_____
_____
_____
_____

EMBARK ON THESE TASKS:
• Have you completed the exercises in this chapter? If yes, what insight(s) did you gain? If no, why not and what is blocking you from doing it?

_____
_____
_____
_____

• Using words, images, ideas, and phrases from your writing, brainstorm about your issue.

_____
_____
_____
_____

Use your journal or a separate paper:
• Draw a picture of your present career, work life, job.
• Draw a picture of your ideal career.
• Write a speech. Imagine this: You are being honored with a lifetime award for your career achievements. Compose a speech summarizing what everyone said about you.

Tool 9: Create an Action Plan

To use an action plan effectively, the rule of thumb is: Less is more. That is to say, a short list of actions you complete will serve you better than creating a long list that remains undone. Taking action is not only empowering, it is psychologically and spiritually uplifting.

When doing Vision work, use as many tools as you can to clarify your passion and imagine doing work you love. This includes reading inspirational books, meditating, creating vision mantras, praying (if you're open to it), listening to podcasts, doing informational interviewing, discussing your hopes and dreams with your Inner Circle, and free associating about your passion.

CHAPTER 20

TOOL 10:
SUBLIMATE YOUR
AGGRESSION

CONVERT YOUR ENERGY
INTO CONSTRUCTIVE ACTION

Throughout the book, there are a number of places I discuss the importance of sublimated aggression. In Chapter 10: The Keys to Success, sublimated aggression is listed as one of the keys to success because it fuels creativity, ambition and consistent action, and is free from conflict, self-sabotage and FOS behaviors.

Tool 10 shows you how to tap into your aggressive drive and convert it into positive, constructive, goal-oriented action. In many ways, you are already doing this. Tool 10 shows you how to do it with conscious intent. Practicing this tool will help you develop the emotional, mental and performance muscles you need to achieve your goals.

Understanding the Aggressive Drive

We are human and we are born with an aggressive drive. It's natural and "built" into our system. At birth, it manifests as crying to get our needs met. Later we act on the environment by reaching for and touching things. As babies we swat at the mobile hanging above the crib, put our toes and other objects in our mouths, turn onto our stomachs, crawl, pull to stand and walk as soon as we are able. We talk. We explore. We initiate. We create. The energy source that gets us to do anything—make a request, reach for an object, build, go toward a goal—is the aggressive drive.

Uncivilized and undisciplined aggression is usually impulsive, reckless and destructive. We see this in children before they learn to use their words and sublimate their aggression. When we convert our aggressive drive into constructive action, attitudes, thoughts and feelings, we gain the ability to go after what we want in constructive ways.

The kind of effort that sustains high performance over time is sublimated aggression working in concert with passion, love and creativity.

However, working with aggression is tricky. As we grow from infancy into childhood and then into adolescence and adulthood, our aggression must grow with us. Over those years, with good guidance, we will learn to sublimate our aggression. That is to say, it will become civilized and disciplined and convert our aggressive drive into constructive words and actions and into creative activities that reflect our passion.

How do we civilize and discipline aggression? When we're young, adults help us. For example, one child might take a truck from another. The child whose truck has been taken away hits that child and the hit child cries. If an adult is near, he or she will intervene. Adults who have good conflict resolution skills will dialogue with the children and work on resolving the conflict constructively without judgment or punishment. Constructive conflict resolution becomes a role model for using sublimated aggression. Imagine the dialogue this way:

Adult (calmly): Why are you crying?

John: Danny hit me.

Danny: John took my truck.

Adult: John, did you take Danny's truck? (John nods affirmatively). I see. We don't hit—we use our words and get help from a grown-up. How about we solve the truck problem this way—John, give the truck back to Danny and when Danny's finished playing with it, he'll give it to you. Will that be okay with you, Danny? (Danny nods affirmatively). Danny, remember, the rule is no hitting. Use your words. If you need help, come to me. I'll help you.

Learning how to use your aggression for constructive communication and action is an essential life skill. Most of us have not sufficiently learned this and it interferes with our life in myriad ways: we stuff our feelings, we hold back in fear, we have difficulty articulating our needs and wants, we express frustration and anger in an indirect or overly aggressive way, and we often have trouble constructing a plan to overcome obstacles. In other words, we resist using our aggression because we don't always know how to convert it into constructive communication or action. Many of us enter adulthood with inefficient coping skills in this area.

To overcome FOS and self-actualize you need sublimated aggression.

Here is the good news: You can convert any form of aggression (nervous aggressive energy, raw aggressive energy, anger, frustration, irritation, annoyance, fury, rage, outrage) into constructive action. When you do, aggression becomes a positive force with positive characteristics that move you progressively forward. In its sublimated form, aggression transforms into these characteristics:

- Ambition
- Assertiveness
- Bravery
- Courage
- Collaboration
- Communication

- Creative action
- Determination
- Faith
- Focused action
- Fortitude to face and overcome obstacles
- Ingenuity
- Persistence
- Risk-taking
- Tenacity
- Willingness to be your authentic and genuine self

Try this exercise: Say each of the above characteristics out loud, one at a time. Then close your eyes and imagine a moment when you were in touch with it. Keeping your eyes closed, let your body feel the aggressive fuel embedded in moments of ambition, determination or creative action.

This exercise helps you get in touch with how our aggressive drive fuels constructive action. Plus, you gain clarity on how much sublimated aggression it takes to be successful.

HIGH PERFORMERS SUBLIMATE THEIR AGGRESSION

Successful people have something in common. They sublimate their aggression to achieve their goals.

To get a better understanding of sublimated aggression, let's look at how one high performer used his aggression positively. Michael Phelps, the Olympic swimmer, is the most decorated Olympian of all time. He won 23 gold medals and 28 medals overall. His trainer Bob Bowman described him as "a solitary man" with a "rigid focus."

To prepare for winning, Bowman described Phelps' training schedule. He said it consisted of swimming and exercise workouts six hours a day, six days a week. To maintain his energy and weight, he ate more than 10,000 calories a day.

A good example of how Phelps sublimated his aggression comes from this story. As a teenager, Phelps idolized Olympic gold-medal swimmer Ian Thorpe. When asked about the likelihood that Phelps would win eight medals in eight events in the 2008 Olympics, Thorpe said it was "highly unlikely." Angered by Thorpe's remark, Phelps taped Thorpe's words to his locker and used them as inspiration to achieve his goals. After Phelps won eight medals in Beijing, Thorpe said, "Never in my life have I been so happy to have been proved wrong."

Practice Sublimating Your Aggression with Your Success Buddy

When your passion gets muted, love for what you do gets dampened, and your aggressive drive is temporarily tied up in FOS Signals, counteract these effects with some sublimated aggression. Create a new Action Plan or renew your old one with your Success Buddy or Group and then *get to work*.

Stay on track by working with your Success Buddy or Group on a weekly basis. Convert what you are experiencing, i.e., discouragement, depression, or despair, into constructive action by creating a simple and doable Action Plan. Start slow. Ten minutes a day will do if you're coming out of a funk or a period of procrastination.

Stay close to your Inner Circle and be in consistent contact with your Success Buddy or Success Group. With group emails and texting, this is easier than ever. If contact with your support people cannot help you move forward, seek help from a therapist or coach knowledgeable in resolving resistances to success and FOS issues.

CHAPTER 21

TOOL 11:
GET YOUR FINANCIAL
LIFE ON TRACK

Your financial life is interwoven with your career and creative endeavors. Tool 11 encourages you to take a deep dive into your relationship to money, earning, spending and saving. While it is all well and good to have a job, you need income that exceeds your monthly expenses to create financial security and peace of mind.

You do not have to be super rich to attain financial security. You can create financial security by handling earning, spending and saving in a reasonable manner. When you stay on track with money and practice healthy financial habits, you gain emotional comfort and serenity.

A number of FOS problems are connected to money issues and money dysfunctions. These include underearning, up and down earnings, under or overspending, shopaholic behavior, being overly focused on material possessions, accumulating debt, illogical attitudes and behaviors with money, and irresponsibility due to grandiosity, depression or a rapid increase in income. Left alone, these money issues will play havoc with your financial life.

While I am not an expert in finance or wealth management, I have developed a set of tips and tools to help my clients face and resolve unhealthy attitudes and habits connected to money. Rethinking your relationship with money is a way to change money dysfunction and how you think about, value and handle money.

The Mothership

I call the family, institution or organization that provided us with food, shelter and clothing in our formative years the *Mothership*. Once we leave the Mothership, there is nothing, absolutely nothing we can do without money. An important developmental task as we enter adulthood is to become self-supporting.

Once you leave the Mothership, you must secure financial resources to function. You can do this by earning your own money or leaning on the support of family, friends, credit cards, personal or business loans, or an institution or organization.

Teens and young adults prepare for the work world by furthering their education, attaining occupational training or entering the workforce straight away.

When you arrive into young adulthood and adulthood with good earning, spending and saving skills, there is a good chance you will secure a job that puts you on the road to financial prosperity. If you arrive into adulthood with poor money habits and earning skills, you are likely to manifest a financial cycle where you survive rather than thrive.

Just surviving rather thriving represents poor self-care and self-sabotage. Tool 11 presents concrete ways to get "right sized" with money. Being right sized takes focus and practice. If you work at it, you can create a happier, healthier and more abundant relationship with earning, spending and saving.

Let's get started.

Money Dysfunction and Stress

Money dysfunction chips away at self-esteem and self-worth. You can avoid becoming trapped in money dysfunction by addressing your issues and creating an Action Plan that helps build new habits.

FINANCIAL STRESS CHECKLIST

Take the Financial Stress Checklist survey if you feel stressed, worried or concerned about money. Check (✔) the box next to each statement that applies to you, even if it applies infrequently:

- ❏ I have fears about money that do not match my financial status.
- ❏ I am underearning and my income does not cover my expenses.
- ❏ I am living above my means.
- ❏ I lack clarity about my income, expenses and savings capacity.
- ❏ I have accumulated debt by using credit cards, taking personal or business loans, or periodically borrowing from family or friends.
- ❏ I overspend.
- ❏ I am a shopaholic.
- ❏ I have irrational fears about money that cause me to be compulsive or illogical with money.
- ❏ I have more money than I need and still feel fearful and unbalanced regarding money.
- ❏ I feel guilty if I save *or* spend money.
- ❏ I have a compulsion to get rid of the money I have.
- ❏ I have financial security and enough money, yet I still feel compelled to make more money and accumulate more material things.

EXERCISE: Write what you discovered from doing the checklist.

How would you define your relationship with money? Interview your partner, family, and close friends if you're curious about what others observe about your relationship to earning, spending and saving. Share what you learn with your Success Buddy.

Trust the Numbers

Getting on track financially depends upon taking a good look at your numbers. This requires taking an inventory of your financial life by assessing your income and expenses, your assets and liabilities.

Contrary to what you might believe, numbers are your friends. Follow your numbers and you will trace your life. Your numbers will give you a clear picture of how you handle earning, spending, and saving. The numbers will also reveal your lifestyle values and the level of financial balance or imbalance you have created in your life.

Assessing your financial picture can be scary and fear can become a resistance to examining your numbers. Don't let FEAR take over! Trust the process. Get clarity on your numbers. If you give the numbers a fair chance, they will lead you to reality, prosperity, progress and self-actualization. Here's how:

GATHER THREE MONTHS OF FINANCIAL DATA

Start by examining your income and expenses for the past three months. Make a comprehensive list of income and expenses. Record every expense, even when you buy a bottle of water or a pack of gum. Take a focused look at what you spend on a monthly basis. Tracking your numbers will give you an accurate idea of your overhead, miscellaneous expenses and the total income you need to live comfortably.

Get clarity on your income and expenses by creating an Income-Expense Worksheet similar to this one:

Sample Income-Expense Worksheet

	January	February	March
Net Income (income after taxes & deductions)			
Jane	2737.50	2737.50	2737.50
Paul	3500.00	3500.00	3500.00
Yearly Bonuses amortized: Jane (2500/yr.) Paul (3500/yr.)	208.33 333.33	208.33 333.33	208.33 333.33
Total Income	**6779.16**	**6779.16**	**6779.16**
Expenses			
Rent or Mortgage	554.40	554.40	554.40
Property Taxes	208.33	208.33	208.33
Home Owners Insurance	55.00	55.00	55.00
Utilities • Electric • Oil/Gas • Boiler Contract • Water • Sanitation	128.00 195.00 15.00 26.00 29.00	128.00 195.00 15.00 26.00 29.00	128.00 195.00 15.00 26.00 29.00
Grounds (lawn/snow removal)	100.00	100.00	100.00
Cable/Internet/Phone Pkg.	110.00	110.00	110.00
Food (groceries, take out/delivery)	800.00	800.00	800.00
Auto • Car Loan • Insurance (for J & P) • Gas • DMV Registration • Upkeep & Maintenance	201.00 216.00 137.00 3.33 25.00	201.00 216.00 137.00 3.33 25.00	201.00 216.00 137.00 3.33 25.00
Medical/Dental • Doctors (co-pays) • Dental (co-pays)	10.00 30.00	10.00 30.00	10.00 30.00
Life Insurance • Jane • Paul	95.00 110.00	95.00 110.00	95.00 110.00
Clothing Allowance • Jane • Paul	75.00(NU) 75.00(NU)	75.00(+75)(NU) 75.00(+75)(NU)	75.00(+150) 75.00(+150)
Personal Allowance • Jane • Paul	500.00 500.00	500.00 500.00	500.00 500.00
Entertainment Allowance (movies, plays, concerts, other)	60.00	60.00	60.00
New and Luxury Categories	Planned in advance as we can afford		
Total Expense	4298.06	4298.06	4298.06
Debt Repayment	205.00	205.00	205.00
	4503.06	**4503.06**	**4503.06**
Money for Miscellaneous Spending-Savings-Investments-Retirement	2276.10	2276.10	2276.10

Jane's 3-Month Income-Expense Worksheet – 2019 / Legend: NU: Not Used - NA: Not Applicable – Amortized (divided by 12 months)

CREATE A REALISTIC SPENDING PLAN

Create a workable spending plan. Start by listing priority categories like rent/mortgage, utilities, food, clothing, laundry, transportation, health insurance and medical/dental/vision expenses. Add cellphone, internet charges and any debt you have. Lastly, add "wish list" items that include expenses you may not have the money for now, but can manifest in the future such as a second honeymoon or a new sofa. Ask family members, friends or co-workers who are "good" with money to give you tips. The resource information in Part IV lists support groups and organizations that can help you with debt and money issues.

EXERCISE: Assess Your Relationship with Money

Write the answers to these questions and share with your Success Buddy:

1. What words and concepts come to mind when you think about money? What does money represent: financial security, unrestricted freedom to purchase, power, status, fame or something to save and never use?
2. Describe your relationship with money. Do you feel happy, joyous and at ease? Or does money create drama, pain, fear, or anger around earning, spending and saving?
3. Make a list of your financial goals and aspirations.
4. Identify the attitudes, beliefs and habits you learned about earning, spending and saving from your parents, family, friends, your community and society.
5. Are you financially solvent (is your income equal to or greater than your expenses)? If your answer is "Yes," describe how you handle income, expenses and savings. If your answer is "No," identify and describe your problem using the prompts below:

a. I believe I have healthy financial habits and live a financially solvent life (describe):

b. I am not financially solvent (describe):
   i. I live paycheck to paycheck and have minimal reserve funds and no savings.
   ii. I am always worried about money and here's why
   _____.
   iii. I underearn and supplement my income by using one or more of these solutions: credit cards; liquidating assets; borrowing money from family, friends, or financial institutions; or accepting financial support from friends and family.

Develop a Healthy Relationship with Money

A healthy relationship with money means handling money in a reasonable way and practicing moderation. Moderation means we don't under- or overspend; we don't deprive or overindulge ourselves.

A healthy relationship with money means living within our means and being thoughtful, generous and prudent regarding finances. When we are in good financial health, we make good use of our money and build financial security to the best of our ability.

Financial security doesn't mean becoming super rich. Financial security means thriving financially instead of surviving. It means earning an income that exceeds your expenses. And, it means living within your means. This is what Buddhists call "the middle way." By living in moderation, you create financial comfort and peace of mind.

Abundance Thinking
vs.
Deprivation Thinking

Ask yourself if you live in fear or faith regarding money. Prosperity thinkers (also called "abundance thinkers") believe there is always enough and more where that came from. They are trusting, generous and willing to share money, knowledge and contacts. They have compassion for others and build rapport and trust easily. They see the bright side and live in faith and optimism. Abundance thinkers believe there are enough resources for all of us to live healthy, safe, fulfilling lives.

Deprivation thinkers (sometimes called "scarcity thinkers") believe resources are limited and there is not enough. They find it difficult to be generous. They often feel withholding and reluctant to share money, knowledge and contacts. They live in fear that they're not going to get something they want or they're going to lose something they have. They tend to be suspicious and untrusting.

Abundance thinking anticipates positive outcomes. Deprivation thinking anticipates negative outcomes or predicts catastrophe or chaos.

Deprivation Thinking is a Trap

Deprivation thinking is discouraging, and emotionally and spiritually depleting. There are a few negative affirmations and attitudes that are guaranteed to keep prosperity beyond your reach. For example: *I never have enough money!* That's a terrible affirmation to use. Another unproductive one is: *Money goes out faster than it comes in.* The Universe can only respond to what you believe about yourself and your life.

Prosperity thinking is empowering and encouraging. It urges you to forge forward and manifest prosperity. Thoughts like *I can embrace new avenues of income! I am worthy of making more money* and *I can do what I love and make an abundant income,* are uplifting.

Rather than stay trapped in deprivation thinking, make prosperity thinking a habit. In this way, you leave deprivation thinking behind and move into an optimistic state of mind that fosters prosperous actions.

The table below illustrates how prosperity and deprivation thinking differ.

Prosperity Thinking vs. Deprivation Thinking

Prosperity Thinking	Deprivation Thinking
• Is FAITH based thinking.	• Is FEAR based thinking.
• Is based on the belief that there is enough and more where that came from.	• Is based on the belief that there is a limited supply of money and resources and not enough for everyone.
• Is positive, supportive and encouraging.	• Is negative, discouraging and non-supportive.
• Rests on the philosophy of expansion, growth, and achievement and the idea that resources can be shared.	• Rests on the philosophy of contraction and a win-lose approach that presupposes there are limited resources that cannot not be shared.
• Inspires you to think of others and pursue goals in service of others.	• Inspires you to be self-focused and pursue self-serving goals.
• Fosters an attitude of gratitude and desire to help others succeed.	• Fosters an attitude of cynicism and one-upmanship and a desire to control others.
• Supports your Vision, even when you fail or falter and need to make a course correction.	• Undermines your Vision especially when you fail or falter.
• Encourages you to trust your intuition and manifest an abundant financial life.	• Discourages your intuition and convinces you that manifesting financial abundance is unrealistic.
• Believes in conflict resolution and there is always a way to work things out.	• Believes in intimidation and power and things work out if you manipulate them to go your way.
• Encourages integrity and values in service of doing what you love and following your bliss.	• Encourages power, status, money and profits at all costs.

What Kind of Thinker Are You?

EXERCISE: Are you an abundance or deprivation thinker?

- Think back to your childhood and adolescence. What did you learn from your parents? Were they abundance or deprivation thinkers?
- Discuss with your Success Buddy whether you are an abundance or deprivation thinker. Assess the kind of actions you take. Are they based on abundance or deprivation thinking?
- Is there anything about your thinking you would like to change? If yes, list what changes you would like to make in your thinking and behavior. If no, list what you are doing and why you are satisfied with your thoughts and behaviors.
- The chart below provides you with examples of prosperity and deprivation messages. Identify the messages you hear. Write them down on the chart. If you need more room, use your journal.

Prosperity Messages vs. Deprivation Messages

Prosperity messages are positive and sound like this:	Deprivation messages are negative and sound like this:
• I can manifest my goals.	• I'll never accomplish my goals.
• I'm on the right track.	• You don't know what you're doing.
• There's enough for everyone.	• There's not enough for me.
• The client is interested in my pitch.	• The client is not interested in what I have to say.
• People helped me and now I can help others.	• I'm not going out of my way for anyone – no one does anything for me.
•	•
•	•
•	•

Tips for Resolving Financial Issues

UNDEREARNING

To solve underearning, make sure you first get your income to equal your monthly expenses. Accomplish this by taking actions to increase your income: ask for a raise; change to a job that pays more money; or take a second job to supplement your income. Once your income covers your basic financial needs, work toward having your income exceed your expenses.

While increasing your income may seem like a daunting task, it is less scary when you create an Action Plan. Make a beginning by discussing your underearning problem with your Success Buddy. Create a reasonable and realistic action plan to increase your income. Be accountable at your weekly meetings.

LIVING BEYOND YOUR MEANS

Living beyond your means can happen at any income level when your expenses exceed your income or cash flow.

To get back on track, rein in your expenses. Create a spending plan and make a budget you commit to follow. Talk with your Success Buddy about your budget and what you spend your money on. Look at how and why you are living beyond your means. Are you accumulating material possessions and luxuries to change your mood or "keep up with the Joneses"? If your answer is "Yes," you may want to discuss the topic of living beyond your means with your Spiritual Partner. You might be trying to fill a void inside you that needs a spiritual or psychological solution.

SHOPAHOLISM

Shopaholics are people who shop addictively and use shopping to change their mood the way alcoholics use alcohol. A shopping addiction is serious.

To curb addictive shopping habits, find healthy substitutes for shopping. Create an Action Plan with your Success Buddy. Join a gym, take up a hobby, do volunteer work, take a course, or meet up with friends for fun activities. If you find you cannot substitute other activities for shopping, seek professional help or join a twelve-step program.

BEING OVERLY FOCUSED ON MATERIAL POSSESSIONS

People focused on accumulating material possessions often use their belongings to mask insecurity or bolster low or unstable self-esteem. Some personalities, in particular, focus on outside displays of status or wealth due to the emptiness and lack of self-worth they feel inside. This represents psychological and spiritual depletion.

Compared to 55 years ago, Americans consume more of everything. We own twice as many cars, eat more sugar yearly and are more focused on accumulating material goods than any other society.

Where has all this consumption gotten us? Let's see! Materialistically, we accumulate things we don't readily use or need. To fix our consumption problem, we rent storage units to house these items or clutter our homes with them. Physically, our health is suffering. As a society, we are overweight and out-of-shape. Diabetes is on the rise, as are other physical ailments.

Are we any happier consuming more? Not really. Depression, anxiety and suicide is on the rise in the adult population as well as in the nine- to fifteen-year-old category. Achieving fame, status and material possessions do not resolve unresolved emotional issues. In fact, just the opposite appears to be true. High performers like Michael Phelps and Lady Gaga have gone public discussing their battle with depression. Prominent high achievers like Robin Williams, Kate Spade and Anthony Bourdain committed suicide at the time in their lives when they seemingly had everything. Accumulating material possessions or achieving validation from the world in the form of fame or status didn't help resolve their internal pain and discontent. If you are overly focused on material possessions, it won't help you either.

Do yourself a favor: do not glorify materialism and feed the fantasy that it will give you a feeling of internal value or happiness. As the Beatles wisely noted, money can't buy us love and we'd do well to remember that it can't buy happiness, a feeling of worthiness or self-love either.

If you are overly focused on material possessions, assess how you feel inside. Do you feel insecure? Do you use your material possessions to bolster your self-esteem or make you feel more interesting or worthy? Are you ignoring that you engage in negative self-talk or the compare-despair game telling yourself *I'm not good enough!* or *If I had what (he/she) has, I'd be* _____ (fill-in the blank).

Unresolved self-esteem issues can be resolved with peer support and therapy. You may not believe it, but the truth is this:

YOU'RE TERRIFIC AS YOU ARE!

Work with your Inner Circle to create an action plan that includes daily meditation, spiritual enhancement, and self-love work.

ACCUMULATING DEBT

Getting into debt is likely to happen if you underearn, live beyond your means, or overspend. Debt means accumulating credit card balances or taking personal or business loans from family, friends or institutions to fill financial gaps. It indicates you are not able to live on your current income.

You can reverse these habits and begin to build healthier ones. To begin, clarify how much you owe. Make a list of each creditor and your monthly payment obligation. If you owe money to family and friends and are not on a payment plan with them, go to them and tell them you are working on creating a payment plan. On the other hand, if you have credit card debt or loans and are struggling to make your monthly payments, you may need to talk with your creditors directly. Some creditors will arrange for a ninety-day moratorium on payments or stop the interest on the credit card bills. Talk with your Success Buddy. You may need professional advice or support from one of the twelve-step programs that address money issues, such as Debtors Anonymous or Underearners Anonymous. You need and deserve good support when you're working with your creditors.

ILLOGICAL ATTITUDES AND BEHAVIORS WITH MONEY

An illogical relationship with money happens when money is handled in a way that does not reflect your financial circumstance and appears out of step with right action. This can happen at any economic level. Poor families can sport new cars and flat screen TVs; rich people can wear raggedy clothes and drive run-down cars.

Interesting examples are the binge-starve pattern sometimes called the over- or underspending pattern. In this money dysfunction, people vacillate between overspending and underspending. While neither side of the pattern represents a realistic or moderate way of handling money, many people do it.

Illogical attitudes and behaviors about money include taking contradictory actions, taking unreasonable actions, justifying the binge-starve pattern, living in a constant state of financial worry and insecurity which does not match the reality, thinking you have more money than you have, and ignoring financial realities.

IRRESPONSIBILITY DUE TO GRANDIOSITY, DEPRESSION OR A RAPID INCREASE IN INCOME

Acting irresponsibly with finances can happen if you slip into states of grandiosity or depression. And, some people are especially at risk when they experience a rapid increase in fame or fortune.

In the grandiose pattern, you feel overly powerful, demanding and arrogant. In this state, it is difficult to make financially sound and prudent decisions. Many people overspend or spend recklessly.

Depressives devalue themselves and experience self-doubt and pessimism. This can trigger underspending and overspending behaviors or an apathetic attitude toward money and materialism.

Being catapulted into financial success can set off a series of irresponsible actions. I have personally worked with people across industry lines who become high earners overnight. Unprepared, they act illogically with money. Instead of being prudent and sensible, they often overspend and over-accumulate. And some vacillate between underspending and overspending depending on their mood.

Work to Improve Your Financial Picture

As soon as you realize you are in financial stress, disengage from unhealthy earning, spending and saving patterns. If you're underearning and your income is not commensurate with your talent, experience or expertise, do something about it. If you have an abundant income and are engaging in a binge-starve pattern, address it now.

Remember, you do not have to be super rich to create financial serenity and happiness.

While money and material possessions will not bring you love, long-term happiness or emotionally fulfilling connections to others, getting healthy with money will bring you peace of mind and freedom from financial insecurity.

Here are a couple of case studies that illustrate unhealthy patterns with money.

Greg

Greg, a successful executive, had a Horatio Alger rags-to-riches story. Over a 25-year period, he rose up the corporate ladder to the C-suite and was in succession for the CEO position.

His creative ideas and ingenious reworking of product sales increased the gross sales of his company by millions. It's no surprise, with his talent, that he became a corporate star with a multimillion-dollar portfolio from salary, bonuses, stock options and good investments.

From the outside, Greg had what I call, the "looking-good" life. He married his high school sweetheart, had five kids, a beautiful house and nice cars. He was well-liked by his neighbors and active in his community.

However, he had deprivation thinking that manifested in an illogical relationship with money, which he inherited from his family. At times he was generous, other times withholding.

Two interactions with his son illustrate his problem. While away at college, Jason asked Greg to deposit money in his checking account for sneakers. He estimated a new pair would cost between $90 and $125, so he requested the higher amount. While he earned money from a part-time job, it was not enough to buy the shoes.

That semester, Jason also requested a new cellphone with a data upgrade. The cellphone carrier told Jason his father would have to pay for a new phone and fax permission for a data upgrade to the family plan.

Weeks passed and Greg did not deposit money for the sneakers, nor did he pay for a new cellphone or fax permission for the data upgrade. Jason called me very upset, requesting a joint session with his father to discuss the matter and his feelings of fear, hurt and anger.

Recapping the phone call he had with his father, Jason told me how he got to the "end of his rope":

"I am so upset. Dad 'grilled' me about money for sneakers asking, 'When was the last time you bought new sneakers?' and 'Do you have to buy sneakers now?' I told him my sneakers had holes in them and he kept going on and on. I think he finally agreed to give me the money because I was very upset on the phone and he never wants me to be angry with him. It's been weeks and he still hasn't deposited the money in my account. As for the cellphone stuff, I started asking him to do this two months ago and he still hasn't taken care of it. He says he's investigating it and will get to it soon. I didn't have the courage to discuss the cellphone, it's too much for me!"

We agreed that a session with his father might move things forward. To prepare for that session, we discussed how money had been handled in the family while he was growing up.

Jason recalled that Greg had always handled money in an "odd way." From an early age, Jason remembered being given a hard time when he asked for money. In contrast, Greg would buy himself expensive things. During the sneaker/cellphone fracas, he paid cash for an expensive car and flew to another state to pick it up.

Greg's illogical relationship with money included discrepancies Jason could not understand. While he bought himself expensive work clothes, at home he walked around in worn-out T-shirts and jeans. In addition, he never questioned his wife's overspending on things she never used. The prior year, she spent more than $200,000 on the shopping network for things that remained unopened in a closet.

These money issues put Jason in conflict with his father, whom he loved deeply. He felt uncomfortable and scared to ask him for anything connected with money. While he did not want to approach him about money, he was still dependent on him.

In the joint session, Greg was defensive and rationalized his behavior. His explanations reflected deprivation thinking and a reservoir of deeply rooted anger. He resented the family spending money he earned, and said, "I can buy myself anything I want because I make the money."

This vignette illustrates how an illogical relationship with money can play out, and how anger and deprivation thinking contribute to the problem. Greg's deprivation thinking and withholding behavior had a negative impact on his family. It didn't stop there. It leaked into his career, proving the old adage "Wherever you go, there you are!"

Today, Greg is more generous, giving, and trusting. He's more open and willing to ask for and accept help. He has improved his relationship with his wife and kids. He and Jason have repaired the parts of their relationship that were broken. If he slips into deprivation thinking, he is open to hearing about it and examining it. He's become teachable. I often remind him that he has adopted the philosophy of *living in faith rather than fear*. He says, "It feels good."

NANCY

Nancy, a 42-year old professional and mother of two, had a vision issue and another form of money dysfunction, vacillating spending. She wavered between deprivation and binge spending.

Nancy and her husband were comfortable financially. He was a high school principal and she taught secondary English. Their two incomes afforded them a nicely decorated home, two cars and money in savings, pensions and small investments.

Nancy was a student in one of the graduate psychology courses I taught at a local university. After she earned her master's degree, she came into supervision with me to learn strategies for resolving resistances in the classroom. I coached her for many years on career, family and unresolved childhood trauma issues.

As our work progressed, Nancy became aware she had given up on her true passion: psychology. Growing up, she dreamed of becoming a psychologist or social worker. When she told her parents she was going to major in psychology they discouraged her. They campaigned for her to become a teacher to ensure she would have a stable income. Wanting their approval, she gave up on her dream and yielded to their vision, telling herself, "Teaching is the safer choice. I'll have a yearly income and benefits with holidays and summers off."

Not realizing it, Nancy kicked her passion to the curb. While teaching was rewarding and some of her work involved psychological interventions, she was not doing what she loved.

Through our work, Nancy revived her passion. She resigned from classroom teaching and transitioned to being a curriculum specialist and educational consultant.

Eventually, Nancy decided to become a psychotherapist. She enrolled in a post-graduate training institute and retooled, reschooled and revamped her career. She became a certified psychoanalytic psychotherapist and went into private practice.

During the years I worked with her, we rarely discussed money. It didn't seem to be an issue. Well into our work, I discovered her deprivation thinking through discussions about her wardrobe. Nancy often wore interesting outfits and sometimes I would take note and compliment her. A frequent response was, "Oh this! It's a hand-me-down from a friend."

Since we were focusing on so many other issues, the phrase *hand-me-down* slipped by me. One winter, her coat caught my attention. She wore a designer coat, very expensive. I knew the coat because I had seen it on the runway the season before and fell in love with the design but not the price. When I said, "That's quite a coat!" Nancy replied, "My friend Marcia gave it to me. She doesn't like it anymore."

Luckily for us, the coat opened the door to discussing her hand-me-down clothes. I learned that she rarely bought her own clothes. A detailed discussion about money revealed that Nancy was vacillating between deprivation and compulsive spending. From a lower middle-class family, she had very few nice things growing up. She described herself as "pretty and popular" and, "on the poor side." Nancy told me her more affluent friends passed their clothes and accessories on to her. That pattern continued into adulthood, long after she needed hand-me-downs. Once we opened the door to the subject of money, Nancy admitted to binge spending at thrift shops and stores like Costco.

When Nancy became aware of her money issues, she worked on developing better spending habits. We created a personal spending plan that included coats, clothes, shoes and jewelry. She bought a designer outfit and an expensive pair of shoes—two luxury items she never would have allowed herself in the past. She addressed her binge spending by adjusting the household budget and curbing her desire to over-buy cases of water, toilet paper and giant packages of food.

Nancy's money story ended happily. Unhealthy money habits were replaced with healthy spending patterns. She practiced abundance thinking and let go of her deprivation mentality. She stopped over-buying and accepting hand-me-down clothes from her friends. When she went into private practice, she was very proud of buying new furniture for her office, and only one case of toilet paper at a time.

Greg's and Nancy's stories illustrate that deprivation thinking interferes with and contributes significantly to money dysfunction. Below is a way to build abundance thinking.

Build Your Prosperity Muscles

Change negative thinking into positive thinking and negative self-talk into positive self-talk. Louise Hay suggests you release negative thoughts about money. "Let them go. They haven't served you well in the past and will not serve you well in the future."

To let go of deprivation thinking, identify your deprivation thoughts and then convert each to an abundance thought. When your list is complete, you can create a release ceremony. Two come to mind: 1) at the beach, write each deprivation thought in the sand and let the waves wash them away; or 2) write each deprivation thought on a small piece of paper and then burn them in a fireplace, burning bowl or safe container.

Deprivation/Scarcity Thinking

CHANGE TO ➤ Abundance/Prosperity Thinking

➤ I'll never accomplish my goals

CHANGE TO ➤ ➤ I can achieve what I set out to do.

➤ The client probably won't buy from me.

CHANGE TO ➤ ➤ The client is interested in my pitch and is likely to want what I'm selling.

➤ I'm not going out of my way for anyone—no one ever does anything for me.

CHANGE TO ➤ ➤ I'm going to bake banana bread and bring it to the office.

Prioritize Financial Problems

It's best to tackle financial problems using a priority system. Confront the most serious issues first. Approach your financial issues the way doctors perform triage in emergency rooms.

PRIORITIZE

1. Address conditions that are causing the most financial pressure:
   a. Underearning
   b. Up and down earnings

      c.   Credit card debt
      d.   Personal or business loans
2.   Financial insecurity characterized by:
      a.   A pervasive feeling of fear and being overwhelmed about money
      b.   A constant struggle to make ends meet
      c.   Never having enough money
      d.   Paying down debt
3.   Identify and handle money dysfunctions such as:
      a.   Under- or overspending
      b.   Money addictions or dysfunctions such as shopaholic behavior, deprivation or binge spending, and an illogical relationship with money

FIRST THINGS FIRST

Underearning is a priority. Work toward getting your income to equal your basic monthly expenses. Focus on increasing your earnings. Take income producing actions. Create an Action Plan with your Success Buddy that moves you toward your goal incrementally. Here are some ideas:

- Ask for a promotion or raise.
- Look for a new job that pays more.
- Take on a second job.
- Move toward your A-Job by taking a B-Job or C-job (Review Chapters 4 (Vision Issues) and 19 (Create an Action Plan)).
- Brainstorm with your Success Buddy about new ways to make money.
- Practice meditating and thinking abundantly.

These tips can help you get started. For the more serious issues, seek advice from financial counselors, mentors or organizations experienced in solving financial problems. They will provide you with the support and guidance you need to turn your financial situation around. For examples of resources see Part IV.

Take Action

Create an Action Plan that includes:

- Thinking abundant/prosperous thoughts.
- Earning an income commensurate with your ability, expertise and experience.
- Creating a financial plan that focuses on short- and long-term goals.
- Creating a realistic spending plan (a budget).
- Making a commitment to stop incurring unsecured debt.
- Creating a repayment plan to retire credit card debt and loans.

Learn How to Build Financial Security

Keep in Mind:

1. Work closely with your Success Buddy.
2. Discuss abundance/prosperity thinking with your support people (Success Buddy, Success Group Spiritual Partner and Inner Circle).
3. Practice abundance thinking.
4. Get clarity on your income and expenses.
5. Stop using credit cards or unsecured loans.
6. Stop deficit spending as soon as possible.
7. Level underearning. Look for a job that pays more and has increased benefits. Get a second job if necessary.
8. Work at your A-Job (doing what you love) if possible.
9. Get a B-Job until you can work full or part time at your A-Job. Your B-Job must provide:
   a. A comfortable salary;
   b. benefits;
   c. a culture that honors and appreciates your talents, expertise and experience;
   d. good working conditions that allow you time to pursue your A-Job on a part-time basis.

10. Level fear, anxiety and negative self-talk by borrowing faith from your Inner Circle: Success Buddy, Spiritual Partner, family, friends and mentors.

11. Find a financial mentor. Learn about earning and finances from someone who has achieved prosperity and created a healthy financial life.

TIPS TO ENHANCE
YOUR PROSPERITY CONSCIOUSNESS

Shoot for the Stars

*Tune into Your Passion * Create a Vision * Do What You Love * Follow Your Bliss*

To move in the direction of your bliss, improve your current situation. If you have any of the money issues mentioned in this chapter, start to turn things around. Investigate making a move within your company. Find a new and creative way to do your job. Suggest to your boss that you take on more responsibilities. Think of transitioning to a new job or career.

Affirm your abundance and be grateful for what you do have. Then focus on expansion. When you focus on deprivation, deprivation shows up in your life. When you focus on abundance, abundance shows up in your life. Think positive thoughts:

- I have enough money.
- I am prosperous.
- I have everything I need.

The more you believe this, the more your physical surroundings will shift to match your expectations.

DO THINGS THAT MAKE YOU HAPPY

When you spend time doing things you enjoy, you automatically feel happier. When you feel happier, you emit positive vibrations, and attract the things you want more quickly and easily. Spend more time doing the things that make you happy: hobbies, socializing with family and friends, and enjoying the small stuff.

STAY CLOSE TO YOUR TRUSTWORTHY SUPPORTERS

Close weekly contact with your Success Buddy, Spiritual Partner, and Success Group will boost self-confidence and help you stay positive and focused on abundance thinking.

CREATE A SOLID ACTION PLAN

Create a financial Action Plan with your Success Buddy to attract abundance in your life. Deepen your spiritual connection. Work to expand your faith by working with your Spiritual Partner to add prayer, meditation and spiritual exercises to your weekly routine. Think of actions that will change your circumstances. Even one small step toward what you want can trigger a flood of opportunities and synchronicities that gets everything moving in the right direction. At the very least, taking action can boost your confidence and make you feel more empowered. Bookend your actions by calling your Success Buddy before you start and after you've finished.

CULTIVATE AN ATTITUDE OF GRATITUDE

An appreciative mindset makes everything better. You will feel more abundant and your focus on the positive aspects of your life will naturally attract more things to be grateful for. Make it a daily habit to appreciate the things that happen. The more you appreciate even the small things, the more you will find good things happening to you.

LOOK FOR SIGNS OF PROSPERITY

Watch for the miracles that come in small signs. You may find money in the street, get a phone call from a friend you haven't heard from in ages, learn of a job opportunity or run into an old client who was thinking of you. The Universe is giving us signs of abundance all the time. Pay attention, and you'll see.

LOVE, LOVE, LOVE

Love is the most powerful and transformational force on the planet. Love yourself, love your family and friends and love the money you have. To reinforce your feelings of prosperity, place small sums of money around the house.

BOOST YOUR SELF-WORTH

Your beliefs have everything to do with the things you experience on a daily basis. If you don't believe you deserve to have prosperity, you will not have it. Tell yourself you are valuable and worth it.

MAKE ROOM FOR MORE

If every nook and cranny of your life is crammed with clutter and disharmony, you have no room for prosperity to come in. One of the quickest ways to get abundance flowing more smoothly through your life is to clear a space for it. Get rid of physical clutter and release painful emotional burdens and unresolved issues. Clean up your physical, spiritual, emotional and financial affairs, and watch how easily they are transformed from stagnant to vibrant.

FOCUS ON EXPANSION

Focus on what you want to expand and attract. Think about your Vision. What you focus on expands. Positive thoughts and emotions will automatically attract more positive circumstances into your life. The more you train your mind to look for blessings and to remain open to possibilities, the more blessings you will see. Start a new positive thinking habit today and watch how it transforms your life.

DIAL DOWN THE BAD NEWS

Turn off the news. Reduce your daily intake of newspaper and magazine articles that report negative things about the economy. Visualize your prosperity and use affirmations to summon what you want to bring into your life.

CONTINUE TO NURTURE YOUR SPIRITUAL SIDE

Expand your spiritual side. Seek inner balance and the presence within that represents your highest and best self. Take a walk or hike in nature, meditate, pray, help others and be generous. These are a few things you can do to get started.

Create prosperity affirmations like these:

- I surrender my financial affairs and concerns about money to divine care and love.
- I ask that my worries, anxieties and fears about money be replaced with faith.
- I know and trust that my debts will be paid, and money will flow into my life.
- I have only to look to nature to see proof of the abundance that is here.

- I erase all negative thoughts about money and know prosperity is mine.
- I am grateful for all that I have in my life.
- I manage my finances wisely, seeking help where needed.

In Summary

Tool 11 encourages you to get your financial life on track by taking a deep dive into your relationship to money, earning, spending and saving. It shows you how to improve and build healthier money habits, adopt abundance thinking and release deprivation thinking. By adopting an abundance mentality you can begin to live in FAITH rather than FEAR.

Tool 11 rests on the philosophy that financial stress and money dysfunction undermines success and interferes with serenity and peace of mind. This tool explains how to resolve money dysfunction by examining your numbers, creating a realistic spending plan and adopting new ways of thinking and behaving. It provides tips on how to address problems such as: underearning, living beyond your means, shopaholism, being overly focused on material possessions, accumulating debt, or illogical attitudes and behaviors around money. It also provides you with a way to begin to prioritize your financial problems and address them one at a time. Lastly, Tool 11 describes how to build financial security and enhance prosperity consciousness.

The importance of this tool and getting your financial life on track should not be underestimated. How you handle money, earning, spending and saving is critical because it is closely interwoven with your career and creative endeavors.

CHAPTER 22

TOOL 12: PREVENT SABOTAGE AT THE TOP

"Happy are they who can hear their detractions and put them to mending."

William Shakespeare
Much Ado About Nothing

Tool 12 is a proactive tool as well as an alert to red flags (early warning signs). When you reach the top levels of success or ascend to the top of your game, it is essential you take precautions to prevent Sabotage at the Top. You can do this by using proactive tools early.

The best times to be proactive are when you are moving into Stages 3 and 4 on the Success Continuum, when you first reach high levels of performance and visibility, and when you are solidly at the top of your game. As we saw earlier, performing reliably and consistently at your personal best is a challenge. To prevent FOS from emerging as Sabotage at the Top, you must be vigilant and watch for small and subtle signs that sound the alarm you are slipping into self-sabotage.

Previously, we looked at the two major patterns to guard against:

grandiosity and depression. Behavioral signs include inconsistent performance, slipping into a "slump" (common in sports), engaging in risky behaviors that disrupt performance, using or abusing substances, or engaging in any behavior that has the potential to derail you.

Prevent Sabotage at the Top, be proactive! Here's how:

Lean on Your Inner Circle

Lean heavily on the people in your Inner Circle. They will help you understand the red flags that signal you are getting off track.

Heed the Early Warning Signs

Early warning signs of Sabotage at the Top are:

- Feeling mild to moderate fear, a pressure to perform, stress, or anxiety that doesn't go away.
- Feeling uncomfortable with increased visibility and acknowledgement.
- Feeling inadequate, unworthy or in danger of being "found out."
- Feeling depressed in response to success and wondering "Is this all there is?"
- Feeling powerful and grandiose, evidenced by making demands, surrounding yourself with an entourage, or feeling arrogant and above the rules.
- Acting on a desire to mute or medicate feelings and thoughts with substances (alcohol, drugs, food).
- Engaging in activities that have the potential to interfere with performance or derail your career: getting involved in an inappropriate romantic or sexual relationship; distracting oneself with screens or social media; and acting irresponsibly

by coming to work late, not showing up at all or performing inconsistently.

These red flag first alerts indicate FOS is activated and they are in the early stages of interfering with your success. A second problem occurs when you or those around you downplay the importance of your uncomfortable feelings. Uncomfortable feelings need to be faced head-on or they become buried or suppressed until they surface as psychological symptoms such as anxiety or frustration or physical symptoms such as back pain or migraine headaches. These symptoms reflect the presence of an emotional conflict often characterized by questions such as, "What can I do to feel better?" and "Everything is going well, why am I feeling this way?"

A third red flag happens when you feel and think at the extremes of the self-esteem continuum. Feeling grandiose or inadequate indicates FOS is operating. These feeling states are the beginning of a downward spiral.

We've looked at some of red flags that can lead to Sabotage at the Top. Review the early warning signs and identify if and when you are experiencing them.

FOS and Sabotage at the Top

Keep in mind the expression, "You are your own worst enemy." It characterizes Sabotage at the Top. Your unconscious creates ways to handle the pressures of success. When you are vulnerable, FOS has a chance to step in. Its objective is to move you away from the cause of your fear (your success) in an attempt to protect you and save you from the dangers of success or from feeling uncomfortable and unsafe. Feeling fear, pressure, stress, anxiety, anger, resentment, and frustration are all connected with feeling uncomfortable and unsafe with success. While success brings many gifts, it is also fraught with peril.

Work with a Specialist

As you are moving through the stages of the Success Continuum, consider working with a professional who has years of experience working with high performers. Find a psychologist, social worker, or coach who has a practice focused on performance enhancement. Work with a professional who has a track record and the expertise to handle the myriad issues that face those reaching for the top and those of you who are already at the top of your game.

Stay Right Sized

Success can go to our heads and inflate our egos. It is important to keep in mind that as you become more and more successful, you need to stay "right sized" and appreciate where you've come from and where you're going. Stay humble. Honor your natural talents. Be vigilant about your character defects and vulnerabilities. They often raise their ugly heads and get you in trouble. Keep your primary purpose in mind. Be of service to others. Share your gift or gifts with the world. My gift is to help others live in their potential and self-actualize. Actors entertain, CEOs lead, mechanics fix, farmers grow food. We all have a job to do, a mission to fulfill. And we can't go to the top of our game and perform at our personal best if we are in our own way.

In his book, *What Got You Here Won't Get You There: How Successful People Become Even More Successful,* Marshall Goldsmith (Goldsmith, Reiter, 2007) pinpoints twenty self-destructive habits that stifle, interfere with or derail those who already have successful careers. His case studies describe high performers, many of whom are CEOs and senior leaders in the corporate world, who under- or overuse their strengths. This clearly leads to what I describe as Sabotage at the Top.

Prevent self-destructive behavior by being proactive and facing yourself honestly. Get to know your strengths, weaknesses and vulnerabilities. Despite our imperfections, we are all magnificent human beings with gifts the planet needs.

My best advice is this: Focus on living in your potential. Pay attention to yourself and lean on your support team.

CHAPTER 23

TOOL 13:
SAFEGUARD YOUR SUCCESS

FOR THOSE WITH FOS:
ASCEND THE LADDER OF SUCCESS SLOWLY

To overcome FOS and perform at a high level reliably and consistently, ascend the ladder of success in small steps with a lot of support. A slow trajectory upward will help you get used to experiencing success. This way, you give yourself a chance to experience living in your potential and getting acclimated to how it feels. A gradual process gets you in touch incrementally with the fear, anxieties and the "high" success fosters. A slow ascent will also help you put in place *new* tools and *new* behaviors that will immunize you against feeling fearful, anxious and unsafe as you live more and more in your potential.

Go slower, to go faster!

For People with High Visibility or People at the Top of Their Game

If you are enjoying success, experiencing high visibility, or at the top of your game in your field, be sure to safeguard your success. Pay attention to the red flags mentioned earlier and build a strong support system of people who have your best interest in mind. Identify the people who are riding on your coattails. Move those people away from your Inner Circle to the Outer Circle or beyond.

Surround Yourself with Support

Lean on your Success Buddy, your Spiritual Partner and the rest of the people in your Inner Circle. They have your back and are invested in your success.

As we discussed earlier in the book, move everyone else to an outer ring. Shift anyone who is inconsistently supportive, ambivalent or toxic away from you.

Be open and add people to your Inner Circle when appropriate. Life finds a way to support your mission and vision. Sometimes an unexpected person can become part of your Inner Circle. It might be your partner, a family member, a friend, a colleague, a neighbor—you never know. To refresh your memory, review Chapter 12: Tool 2: Create A Circle of Support and the COS diagram.

Stay in Touch with Your Feelings

It's important to stay in touch with your feelings and identify those that trigger FOS. Continue to do a daily Feeling Check-in—three to four times a day is ideal. It only takes a few seconds to get a read on your emotional clock. Keep it simple! Some people find it helpful to copy and miniaturize the feeling chart and keep it with them. If you practice doing a Feeling Check-in daily, it will become part of your regular routine.

Be vigilant and consistent about taking your emotional temperature. Share your emotions with your Success Buddy and Spiritual Partner. Remember, it's not just negative feelings that catapult you into an emotional puddle. Positive feelings can too!

Moving up the Success Continuum often engenders fear, anxiety, and apprehension. It also elicits feelings of joy, passion, excitement, accomplishment and competence. Both negative and positive feelings can trigger emotional puddles that have the potential to ignite a cascade of self-destructive behaviors. Be vigilant and watch for very small signs that are forerunners of self-sabotage.

SUCCESS, VISIBILITY AND VULNERABILITY

For people with FOS, visibility and success often engenders fear and discomfort. The discomfort stems from increased visibility, moving closer to your goal or reaching the top of your game. The more visible you are, the more you are on other peoples' radar. The more you are on peoples' radar, the more you are exposed to negative consequences.

PEOPLE WITH FOS FEAR:

- Disapproval and negative judgment, directly or indirectly.
- People feeling angry, jealous, envious or competitive with their success.
- People feeling toxic envy with the aim of taking you down or wanting to take your place.

POSITIVE FEEDBACK CAN ALSO TRIGGER ANXIETY, UNRESOLVED TRUST AND SELF-ESTEEM ISSUES, PERFECTIONISM, AND A PRESSURE TO PERFORM. THESE MANIFEST AS:

- Distrust for the person or organization delivering the positive feedback.

- Poor self-care.
- Self-doubt and negative self-talk.
- Devaluing one's talent and achievement.
- Procrastination and perfectionism.
- Unresolved aggression issues.

A natural response to feeling frightened, vulnerable or exposed, is to create a wall of protection. The unconscious does it for you automatically, when it senses you feel threatened. Just as a country will deploy troops to protect its borders from invasion, we protect ourselves from danger by using our defense mechanisms.

DEFENSE MECHANISMS IN THE FORM OF FOS SIGNALS ARE DEPLOYED BY THE UNCONSCIOUS AND ACT PRIMITIVELY BY PUTTING US INTO ONE OF THESE MODES:

- Flight
- Fight
- Freeze
- Hide
- Play dead

YOUR UNCONSCIOUS DEFENDS YOU 24/7

Among its many duties, the unconscious acts as your personal body-guard. Its job is to be vigilant and monitor your emotional system for signs of danger. It operates instinctively and has a rapid response system that will come to your aid in danger—real or imagined.

Unfortunately, the unconscious is not very good at distinguishing between real danger and imagined danger. Its main purpose is protection. If you feel scared, your unconscious will deploy a defense to protect you.

The unconscious uses defense mechanisms such as denial, repression, suppression, turning aggression against the self (a defense characterized by self-blame and self-criticism), and other techniques to ward off thoughts, feelings and perceptions that make you uncomfortable.

Therefore, if pursuing your dream and achieving or approaching success makes you feel uncomfortable, frightened or panicked, the unconscious will come to your aid. Don't let it get the best of you. Use your tools to keep moving forward.

Use Your Support System

Lean on your support people. Check in with your feelings. Call your Success Buddy, Spiritual Partner, or people in your Inner Circle when you:

- Feel uncomfortable, anxious, threatened, overwhelmed or resentful.
- Sense you are about to engage in one or more of the FOS Signals.
- Notice you're using a defensive mechanism like flight, fight, freeze, hide or play dead.

If you allow your unconscious to drive the "solution" to your fear or discomfort, you'll be in a situation that is difficult to monitor and control. Fear depletes us. When we feel any form of fear, we cannot perform at our best. If you don't get a handle on it early, fear will activate FOS and you will begin to sabotage your efforts, lowering your chances of performing consistently and reaching your goals.

Forewarned is forearmed. At this point, you know your FOS patterns and the signals you use to manifest those patterns. Anticipate they will go into action automatically. Press the "pause" button. Be prepared and be vigilant!

Some of us are great at beginnings. We come out of the gate raring to go and do well in the beginning, but after developing some measure of success, we falter. So, good starters, beware! FOS usually gets activated when we're in Stage 1, 2, or 3 of the success zone. Watch for this and get help to climb to the top tiers.

CHAPTER 24

Tool 14:
Teach What You Know—
Pay It Forward

The best way to keep what you have is to give it away. Teach what you've learned. Pass on what you know to people who want to resolve their career blocks and get out of their own way. Encourage them to do the Inside Job. Inspire them to live up to their potential. Rouse them to tune into their passion, do what they love, and follow their bliss.

When we begin living in our potential, we are clear about our passion and purpose. We use our talents to do what we love. The Inside Job provides you with tools you can pass on to others.

Teaching Others and
Paying It Forward Works

Living up to your potential allows you to live in a state of emotional well-being, gratitude and abundance. From this state, the generosity of doing a good deed for someone else follows naturally. The concept called "pay it forward" is a reflection of the gratitude we experience when we acknowledge that we have benefited from working with those in our Inner Circle, including our Success Buddy, Success Group, and Spiritual Partner. Their kindness, care, mentoring, time, and attention is a gift you can pass on to others. The "pay it forward" method is a way to give to others what has been so generously been given to you.

Paying It Forward

The concept *Pay it Forward* has been around a long time. It can be traced as far back as 317 BC in ancient Greece when Meander wrote his comedy, *Dyskolos* (The Grouch). A key component of the plot was *pay it forward*. Likewise, contract law uses the construct when a creditor offers the debtor the option of paying the debt forward by lending it to a third person instead of paying it back to the original creditor. Repayment of the debt can be monetary or done by good deeds. An extension of this in many modern court systems is to assign offenders to community service.

In 1944, the concept was discussed by a spokesman for Alcoholics Anonymous in the *Christian Science Monitor*. The author wrote, "You can't pay anyone back . . . so you try to find someone you can pay forward."

Oprah Winfrey demonstrated the concept to her television audience in October 2006 when she gave her audience members the opportunity to experience "truly the best gift—the gift of giving back." That day, her studio audience of about 300 people each received a $1,000 debit card. They were instructed to donate all the money to a charitable cause of their choice. The challenge was to make the donation within a week. Armed with their debit cards (and with video cameras documenting their good deeds), they made headlines from Connecticut to California. In a short time, the practice snowballed into a nationwide movement known as Random Acts of Kindness.

It Begins with One Change

It takes courage to embark on a journey to understand and overcome self-sabotage. It takes daring to explore the psychological dynamics involved in playing small. It takes nerve and valor to understand how FOS interferes with your career and creative endeavors.

When you change yourself, you are creating a ripple effect of change in the Universe. Your growth inspires others to do the same. Pay it forward by passing on what you know.

How to Pay It Forward

- Make time to help others.
- Tell your story.
- Discuss the benefits of working with a Success Buddy and Spiritual Partner.
- Discuss how FOS can interfere with or derail success.
- Be a role model for abundance thinking.
- Discuss how crucial it is to:
  a. Tune into your passion.
  b. Get in touch with what you love to do.
  c. Do what you love.
  d. Follow your bliss.
  e. Transition to following a second or third "bliss" if your path leads you there.
- Shine a beacon of hope.

Encourage Vision and Mission

When you work with others, encourage them to acknowledge and value their innate talents, skills and abilities. Encourage them to cultivate their Vision and mission. Keep this in the forefront of your mind while working with people.

Life will provide opportunities for you to do random acts of service. Look for the signs. They will always be there.

BE PRUDENT

Helping others can be a tricky business. Some people are ready, and some are not. When you want to share what you know, remind yourself to be patient and compassionate. *Pay it forward* is meant to be a loving process, a gift to your fellows.

When you recognize that FOS is part of someone's work story or history and you see the FOS symptoms, proceed gingerly. Control your therapeutic zeal, your impulse to be helpful and provide a solution.

First, listen! Assess if some aspect of your story dovetails with your friend's. Like most, your friend may not be conscious of self-sabotage. Over the years, most people I have encountered are not aware FOS is interfering with their career or creative endeavors.

It has been my experience that most people with FOS argue vehemently against that characterization. While they identify their FOS symptoms accurately and are acutely aware they are underearning, underachieving, performing inconsistently, have Vision issues or are engaging in Sabotage at the Top; they rebuff the idea that something called Fear of Success is the cause.

Therefore, when you are presented with an opportunity to tell your FOS story, tell it simply. Describe how you came to recognize FOS. Say something about your progress, what you've learned about FOS and your relationships with your Success Buddy and Spiritual Partner.

Remember, when we pay it forward, we allow our splendor to show and we help others to do the same. When we share our passion, creativity, enthusiasm and excitement, we give others permission to share theirs, too! When we sprinkle hope everywhere we go, we spread the faith that each of us can live up to our potential. It is an idea that is contagious. It is an idea that works.

PART IV

SUMMARY AND RESOURCES

CHAPTER 25

IN CONCLUSION: YOUR CHANGE IS EXCITED TO MEET YOU

We are at the end of our journey together. Thank you for staying the course and completing this work with me. It's not easy to face FOS and make a commitment to do the hard work necessary to make progress. Ultimately, the Inside Job is an act of self-care.

It takes courage to face ourselves honestly and commit to change. The journey is a pilgrimage of self-love. The Inside Job is ultimately about tuning into your passion, doing what you love and following your bliss. This is possible if you get out of your own way and resolve any obstacle that prevents you from following your dream and living in your potential.

It is impossible to solve a problem if you don't know it's there. You cannot change any behavior that is outside your awareness. When you committed to do the Inside Job, you accepted the challenges that come with facing how and why you were stuck in your career and creative endeavors. To accomplish this, you ventured into the arena of the unconscious and worked at making the unconscious conscious.

I know you have changed,
and your
change is excited to meet you.

It is my hope that reading this book, doing the Inside Job exercises, working with a Success Buddy, a Spiritual Partner, and Support Group, and creating a trustworthy Inner Circle, have helped you reach a new level of awareness about how FOS holds you back.

Throughout this journey you were exposed to new information, given the opportunity to practice new behaviors, and learned tools and strategies to help you move forward.

Continue to lean on your Inner Circle and move people to the outer rings when needed. The work you do with them will deepen. Together, you will accomplish what you could not do alone. Your Inner Circle, which includes your Success Buddy and Spiritual Partner, will help you stay on course and keep you focused on your vision and mission. Isolation and loneliness will melt away.

In your Success Buddy, Spiritual Partner, and Inner Circle you have more than friends, you have lifelines. They are dedicated to helping you live your best life. You are no longer alone.

What You Know Now

Right now, you have a clearer understanding of how FOS and how self-sabotage operates in your life. You have a toolbox filled with strategies and interventions for overcoming your FOS Signals and handling feelings such as fear, anxiety, joy, excitement and passion without self-sabotage.

In addition to peer support, some of you have started working with a performance enhancement coach or a psychologist who specializes in re-solving resistances to success. If you have hired an experienced profession-al, it is a gift that will have short- and long-term benefits. First, the profes-sional is trained to identify career blocks and can help you get through any denial or rationalizations that might prevent you from working on them. Second, an experienced coach or psychologist has extensive resources for resolving these kinds of issues. Third, the professional is a step removed from you, from your blocks and from your work life and, therefore, can serve as an objective sounding board to your problems.

Encourage Others

We all struggle with one thing or another. You know how painful it is to be stuck. By reading the book, creating an Inner Circle, working with your Success Buddy and Spiritual Partner, you have experienced first-hand what it's like to have trustworthy support and to move forward. Help others to do the same. Give away what you know.

With your new-found knowledge and an expanded toolkit, encourage those around you to tune into their natural talents and share their gifts with others. Urge them to focus on what they love to do. Tell them it is possible. Give them hope.

Often, we find ourselves teaching what we need to know and learning from those we're guiding. Pay it forward; pass on to others what you have learned.

Be the Change

You can't give away what you don't have. If you want to help the planet, be the change you want to see.

The biggest change we can all make is to honor our natural gifts and help others to do the same. When we allow ourselves to blossom and live in our potential, we give others permission to do the same. When we blossom, we spread beauty, creativity, enthusiasm and excitement. We live in the possibilities. We live in faith and hope. And believe me, it's contagious.

The Inside Job is about positive movement and change. It's been my pleasure to be on this journey with you. I sincerely hope that you have overcome some of your FOS issues, have a close relationship with your Inner Circle, Success Buddy and Spiritual Partner, and are happily on your way to doing what you love and following your bliss. I wish you success in all you do.

And, please stay in touch on our website:

www.successisaninsidejob.com

Let me know how you're progressing, what your struggles are and how you are paying it forward and helping others.

Warmest regards,
Judith F. Chusid

CHAPTER 26

RESOURCES

INFORMATION ABOUT RESOURCES

These resources are provided as information only. Dr. Chusid does not endorse any specific program, organization, or book. The resources are on the list as references for the reader.

Dr. Chusid suggests you inquire about programs and check references and reviews. Ask admissions counselors and program directors if you can speak to prior clients or workshop participants. Always use good judgment and discretion when selecting any of the resources provided.

Accordingly, Dr. Chusid cannot be held liable for the accuracy of this information, nor for the quality of services rendered. The treatment, workshop, and twelve-step programs, as well as the other resources listed below may help make your recovery, self-discovery or educational journey a successful one. There is a great deal of information and help available, and we hope that you will take the first step and reach out for help if you need support to face and overcome addictive behaviors, chemical dependency, substance abuse, sexual and relationship issues, codependency, and trauma and grief issues.

WORKSHOPS FOR SELF-GROWTH

Breakthrough@Caron
844 271-1185
www.caron.org

Personal growth, codependency, ACOA/Dysfunctional Families issues

Esalen Institute
888 837-2536
www.esalen.org

Workshops on relationships, spirituality, self-growth

Kripala
866 200-5203
www.kripalu.org

Workshops on yoga, creative expression, heath-fitness-wellness, self-discovery, spiritual practice and meditation.

Omega Institute
877 944-2002
www.eomega.org

A variety of educational workshops for mind, body, spirit and heart. Annual leadership conference for Women.

Onsite Workshops
800 341-7432
www.onsiteworkshops.com

Experiential workshops to help individuals and couples
experience a breakthrough from being stuck in unhealthy
relationship patterns with self and others.
800 877-4520 Call for info

The Meadows Workshops
866-582-9850
www.themeadows.com

Experiential workshops for individuals, couples and
professionals on a variety of topics such as: codependency,
childhood trauma, women's and men's issues, grief, love
addiction/love avoidance, and sex and love addiction.

Success Is An Inside Job® Workshops
212 463-0080
www.successisaninsidejob.com

Educational and experiential workshops to help individuals,
groups and teams resolve career blocks, confusion about
vision/mission, resistances to success, and fear of success
issues.

Residential Programs

Caron
800 678-2332
www.caron.org

Gender separate residential, primary and extended care rehab for teens, young adults, adults, older adults with drug or alcohol addiction.

Cottonwood
800 877-4520
www.cottonwooddetucson.com

Substance abuse, eating disorders, trauma, adolescent girls program.

The Meadows
800 244-4949
www.themeadows.com

Substance abuse and processing disorders, trauma, depression, co-occurring disorders.

Gentle Path at the Meadows
866 904-4879
www.gentlepathmeadows.com

Sexual additions, emotional trauma, co-occurring disorders

Willow House for Women at the Meadows
877 978-3511
www.willowhouseforwomen.com

Relationship healing for women from love, sex, intimacy issues.

TWELVE-STEP PROGRAMS

Alcoholics Anonymous
www.aa.org

Debtors Anonymous
debtorsanonymous.org

Underearners Anonymous
underearnersanonymous.org

Adult Children of Alcoholics/Dysfunctional Families
adultchildren.org

Al-Anon/Alateen
al-anon.org

Sexual Recovery Anonymous
sexualrecovery.org

Sex and Love Addicts Anonymous
slaafws.org

Sexual Compulsives Anonymous
sca-recovery.org

Notes

Introduction

Sinetar, Marsha, *Do What You Love and The Money Will Follow*, Paulist Press, 1987; Random House, 1989.

Pressfield, Steven, *The War of Art*, Black Irish Books, 2002.

Cohen, N. W., *Explorations in the fear of success*. Unpublished doctoral dissertation, Columbia University, New York, 1974.

Chusid, Judith, "Modern Psychoanalytic Concepts Applied to a Men's Collegiate Lacrosse Team". Final Research Paper for The Center for Modern Psychoanalytic Studies, NY, NY, 1980.

Doherty, Paul, *The History of Adelphi Lacrosse*

Williamson, Marianne, *A Return to Love,* HarperCollins, 1992.

Chapter 1: What is Success? What is Fear of Success?

Pressfield, Steven, *The War of Art*. Black Irish Books, 2002.

McCorvey, J.J., "The Key to Oprah Winfrey's Success: Radical Focus" *Fast Company*, November Issue, 2015.

Sinetar, Marsha, *Do What You Love and The Money Will Follow*, Paulist Press, 1987; Random House, 1989, p. 10.

Scorsese, Martin, *Public Speaking*, HBO Documentary Films, 2010.

Lewin, Kurt, *A Dynamic Theory of Personality,* McGraw-Hill, 1935.

Freud, Sigmund, "Some Character Types Met with in Psychoanalytic Work", *The Standard Edition of the Complete Psychological Works of Sigmund Freud*, Vol. XIV (1914–1916).

Horner, Matina, "Sex and Success", *Time*, March 20, 1972.

Horner, Matina, "Toward an understanding of achievement-related conflicts in women", *Journal of Social Issues* 28 (2), pgs. 157–175, Summer, 1972.

Canavan-Gumpert, Donnah, Garner, Katherine, & Gumpert, Peter, *The Success Fearing Personality: Theory and Research*, Lexington Books, D.C. Heath and Co., 1978.

Chusid, Judith, "Modern Psychoanalytic Concepts in a Men's Lacrosse Team". A Final Paper for the Certificate of Psychoanalysis: The Center for Modern Psychoanalysis, New York, NY, 1980.

Chapter 3: Fear of Success Personality Traits, Patterns & Symptoms

Klein, Melanie, "Envy and Gratitude and Other Works: 1946–1963", *The Writings of Melanie Klein*, Vol. 3. Hogarth Press, 1975.

Chapter 4: Vision Issues

Schwartz, Tony & Porath, Christine: "Why You Hate Work", *The New York Times*, May 30, 2014.

The Power of the Myth with Bill Moyers, Episode 4: "Sacrifice and Bliss", PBS, 1988.

Lewis, Sinclair, *Babbitt*, Harcourt, Brace & Co., 1922.

marianne.com

chopracentermeditation.com (accessed 8/4/17)

Salzberg, Sharon, *Real Love*, FlatIron Books, NY, NY, 2017.

MacFarlane, Seth and Zuckerman, David, *Family Guy*, 1999–2017.

Rilke, Rainer Maria and Kappus, Franz Xavier, *Letters to a Young Poet; Briefe an einen jungen Dichter Insel Verlag*, Leipzig, 1929.

Chapter 6: Underachieving

Smutney, Joan Franklin, "Meeting the needs of gifted underachievers—individually", published by *2eNewsletter*, 2004.

Whitmore, JR, *Giftedness, conflict and underachievement*, Allyn & Bacon, Boston, 1980.

Chapter 7: Workaholism

Robinson, Bryan E, *Chained to the Desk: A Guidebook for Workaholics, Their Partners and Children, and the Clinicians Who Treat Them*, New York University Press, 1988.

Schor, Juliet B., *The Overworked American: The Unexpected Decline of Leisure*, Basic Books, 1991.

Goodman, Brenda, "A Field Guide to the Workaholic", *Psychology Today*, May 1, 2006.

Clark, M.A., Lelchook, A.M., & Taylor, M L., "Beyond the Big Five: How narcissism, perfectionism, and dispositional affect relate to workaholism", *Personality and Individual Differences*, Vol. 8, 786–791, 2010.

Chapter 8: Sabotage at the Top

Collins, James C, *How the Mighty Fall: And Why Some Companies Never Give In*, Random House, 2009.

Chapter 10: The Keys to Success

Newton, Isaac, "Letter to Robert Hooke", 1676.

Chopra, Deepak, *The Seven Spiritual Laws of Success: A Practical Guide to the Fulfillment of Your Dreams*, Amber-Allen Publishing, 2010.

Roosevelt, Franklin Delano, First inaugural address, March 4, 1933.

Chapter 11: Tool 1: Work with a Success Buddy

Star Wars: Episode V—*The Empire Strikes Back*, Lucas Films, 1980.

Chapter 13: Tool 3: Nurture Your Spirit and Body

"Juvenal", Satire X's verse 10.345–64 written ca 120 CE 0.345–64. Translates as "healthy mind in a healthy body."

Bennington, Emily, *Miracles at Work: Turning Inner Guidance into Outer Influence*, published by Sounds True, Louisville, Colorado, 2017.

marianne.com

Thoreau, Henry D, *Walden*, Ticknor and Fields, Boston,1854.

Fillmore, Charles, *Prosperity – Spiritual Secrets to an Abundant Life*, Dover Publications, 2012.

Butterworth, Eric, *Spiritual Economics, The Principles and Process of True Prosperity*, Unity Books, Unity Village, MO, 2001.

CHAPTER 14: TOOL 4: PRACTICE THE 5AS: AWARENESS, ACCEPTANCE, ACTION, ACCOUNTABILITY, ACTUALIZATION

Kelly, Walt, *Pogo* comic, July 20, 1975.

Piaget, Jean, *The Language and Thought of the Child*, Routledge & Kegan Paul, London, 1923.

Schuller, Robert, *Tough Times Don't Last but Tough People Do*, Bantam Books, 1984.

CHAPTER 15: TOOL 5: DO A FEELING CHECK-IN

"Anxiety in the West: Is It Increasing in the US?", Medical News Today, September 5, 2018.

CHAPTER 17: TOOL 7: CLARIFY YOUR VISION

Lao-tzu, *Daodejing* (*Tao Te Ching*), 5th–6th Century BCE.

Moncur, Michael, "The Quotations Page", September 1, 2004.

CHAPTER 21: TOOL 11: GET YOUR FINANCIAL LIFE ON TRACK

Hay, Louise, "Prosperity" quote from louisehay.com. Click Prosperity button: louisehay.com/wisdom-from-louise/topics/prosperity/.

Chapter 22: Tool 12: Prevent Sabotage at the Top

Goldsmith, Marshall with Reiter, Mark, *What Got You Here, Won't Get You There: How Successful People Become Even More Successful*, Hatchett Books, 2007.

About the Author

Judith Chusid, Ph.D. is a therapist, teacher, consultant, qualitative researcher, speaker and workshop facilitator with over forty years of experience. Nicknamed "The Resistance Buster," Dr. Chusid's extensive Toolkit includes strategies for resolving resistances to success and change, fear of success issues, team building and leadership development. She earned her masters and doctorate degrees from New York University, and a Professional Diploma from St. John's University in School Psychology/Professional Child Psychology. She received her post-graduate training from The Center for Modern Psychoanalytic Studies. She was a full-time instructor at Adelphi University and got her start as a sports psychologist with The Panthers, Adephi University's Men's Lacrosse Team.

www.ingramcontent.com/pod-product-compliance
Lightning Source LLC
Chambersburg PA
CBHW071330210326
41597CB00015B/1400